I0568873

WHISTLES AND WISDOM

WHISTLES AND WISDOM

LESSONS ON LIFE AND LEADERSHIP FROM AN SEC FOOTBALL OFFICIAL

CHRIS GARNER

WHISTLES AND WISDOM
Lessons on Life and Leadership from an SEC Football Official

Copyright © 2025 by Chris Garner

All rights reserved. No part of this book may be reproduced, distributed, or transmitted in any form or by any means, including photocopying, recording, or other electronic or mechanical methods, without the written permission from the publisher or author, except as permitted by U.S. copyright law or in the case of brief quotations embodied in a book review.

Disclaimer: Although the publisher and the author have made every effort to ensure that the information in this book was correct at press time and while this publication is designed to provide accurate information in regard to the subject matter covered, the publisher and the author assume no responsibility for errors, inaccuracies, omissions, or any other inconsistencies herein and hereby disclaim any liability to any party for any loss, damage, or disruption caused by errors or omissions, whether such errors or omissions result from negligence, accident, or any other cause.

Interior Layout and Design by Abigael Elliott
Book Cover Design by Stephanie Anderson

ISBNs:
979-8-89165-203-3 *Paperback*
979-8-89165-204-0 *Hardback*
979-8-89165-202-6 *E-book*

Published by:
Streamline Books
Kansas City, MO
streamlinebookspublishing.com

*To my children, Hanna, Jonathan, and Olivia—there
is truly no greater joy than watching you grow, develop,
and become outstanding individuals in what you do. You
have always driven my passion to be better every day.*

*My wife, Anna—you are the one person who has brought
love, peace, comfort, stability, and calmness into my life.*

Mom—without you, none of this would've been possible.

⌐CONTENTS

Introduction IX

PART 1: FALSE STARTS AND BIG GAINS 1

1   Early Losses 3

2   Fourth and Long 13

3   Forward Progress 21

4   Taking the Field 31

5   The Biggest Stage 43

6   Officiating FAQ 55

PART 2: LESSONS FROM THE FIELD 79

7   Relationships 81

8   Preparation 93

9   Communication 111

10 Patience 123

11 Embrace the Grind 133

Acknowledgments 139

About the Author 143

INTRODUCTION

I WROTE THIS book for two reasons. First, I have learned tremendous life lessons from the sport of football in general—from coaching it to officiating it to studying its leadership components. Second, whenever I speak, whether at a large sales conference kickoff or a small business meeting around a table, the first questions people ask me are usually: "Where are you this weekend?", "Where were you last weekend?", and "Were you the one who screwed up that call in that one game?"

On the morning of Sunday, September 15, 2024, I was sitting in the airport in Lexington, Kentucky. Our crew had just worked the Kentucky-Georgia game the night before. The unranked Kentucky Wildcats were beating the No. 1-ranked Bulldogs the entire game until Georgia scored a touchdown in the fourth quarter to survive and win. As I do every Sunday morning, I opened up my laptop and began to scrutinize the game film.

Soon, a woman sat down next to me in the only seat available. She took quite an interest in what was on my computer screen. As I sensed her leaning closer and closer, I noticed her sparkly fan gear.

She asked me if I went to the game. "Yes," I replied, in a single word. She asked me which team I rooted for. I gave her another single-word response: "Neither." That always puzzles people. Then she informed me she was the mother of the star player of the Georgia Bulldogs.

As I write this, I'm not sure how that player's season will end or the total of his accolades, but I've worked enough of his games to know that he is a tough kid and a winner. I've never seen him lose his cool or complain in any game of his that I've worked or watched. He would get knocked down, keep getting up, move his team down the field, and beat his opponent. When his mother shared her identity with me, it gave me some level of comfort. "I'm this guy," I said, and I pointed to my laptop screen, at a striped shirt on the field. Her eyes grew super big. "Okay," she said. "I have all sorts of questions for you."

She and I went back and forth for a solid hour. She was the mother of one of the top players in college football who was playing on, at the time, the No. 1 team in the country. She knew her son's football practice and school schedules, how hard he worked off the field, everything about the team, and how the head coach operated it. She definitely had an inner knowledge of college football. And yet, she asked me questions for nearly an hour. It was simply another confirmation to me that people want to know more about what football officials actually do.

I used to rarely talk about my job, but in a great many cases, it's all that many people want to hear about when they talk to me. So, why fight it? Once, at a Big Ten football clinic, a referee named Alex Kemp (formerly of the Big Ten, now in the NFL) advised how to make announcements during fouls and other administrative stops. He said, "Give the people and fans what they want. They want to know what exactly is going on." Since then, I have learned they want to know about it all day, every day, not just on the day the game is played.

So, let's do that.

You may think being a football official is all about calling holding, pass interference, and touchdowns. The truth is, officiating is really about struggle and determination. Each game averages close to 200 plays or, as we call them, snaps. Of those, 150 to 160 of them are *almost* holding, *almost* an illegal shift, *almost* a delay of game, or *almost* pass interference. Everything is on the edge. The real battle is to hang in there and stay absolutely determined to not get fooled and call only the things that matter. Our job is to manage the game to ensure it runs as efficiently as possible.

I remember the situation that triggered my change in attitude and prompted me to talk more openly about how college football officiating works. In 2017, a passionate football fan in the Southeast asked me, "How does it work? Does Nick Saban call you on Saturday morning and ask you if you can work his game later that afternoon?"

Honestly, I was caught off guard by the lopsided nature of both the question and this person's belief. Nothing could be further from the truth. No head coach in college football calls me or any other official for anything, ever. People outside of officiating circles believe all sorts of wild ideas, rumors, and conspiracy theories. The fan's question put me on alert that many fans may think and believe the same thing. Since then, I've been happy to share with anyone about how it works.

I hope this book strengthens the framework you use to be successful in life. No matter what you do or where you do it, I believe the life lessons I have learned from the world of officiating college football can apply to you in some way.

My sincerest wishes to you in your pursuit of achieving all you want. Everything is possible. Believing it is everything.

PART 1

FALSE STARTS
AND BIG GAINS

CHAPTER 1

EARLY LOSSES

MY GRANDFATHER ALWAYS read the instructions.

It didn't matter if he was building components of a fighter jet or using a toaster. No matter what he was working with, he always wanted to understand how it worked and why it worked that way. "Grandpa," I'd say to him, "it's just a toaster. You put in the bread, and you push down the handle. That's it."

But that wasn't good enough for him. In every single thing he did, he was thorough, hardworking, and determined to understand it from top to bottom, front to back.

I spent a lot of time with my grandparents when I was growing up in Ohio. My parents divorced when I was a toddler, so my mom had to raise me by herself, and she leaned on her parents for support. They picked me up from school, watched me while she was at work, and helped out however they could so she could take care of me.

That meant for several years, I practically lived with my grandparents, especially during the summer. And I loved it. I would beg my mom to go to their house, beg her to let me spend the night, and then beg her to let me stay longer when she came to pick me up. All the time I spent with them gave me the chance to get to know my grandfather better, absorb some of his wisdom, and learn about how he approached his life and work. He was a hero to me, and in my eyes, there was nothing he couldn't do.

My grandfather owned his own home inspection business, so he knew how things worked in a house—the basics of wiring, construction, plumbing, landscaping, and more. He built a brick patio at our house in 1982 that's still intact to this day, as solid as when he built it. He bought a riding lawn mower in the late 1970s that still looked and operated like it was brand new in the late 1990s. Prior to owning his own business, he worked for the defense firm Rockwell International building fighter jets. He had a great, process-oriented mechanical engineering mind. I can't begin to tell you how many times he would ask me if I checked the oil before I cranked up anything that had a motor. If a project required a power tool, measuring tape, or a screwdriver, he knew how to excel at it. It seemed like everything my grandfather did, he did better than anybody else.

He was born in 1921, right before the Great Depression hit in 1929, and he enlisted in the military during World War II, where he served as a pilot. After the war, he went to The Ohio State University and earned his diploma, which he had imprinted on a bronze plate and displayed prominently in his office. Every time I went to my grandparents' house, I would go into his office to look at that diploma, just to make sure it was still there. Even as a young child, I had an appreciation for history and understood how significant it was that he went to college and made something of himself after growing up during the Depression. It was more than just a symbol of his education—it was evidence of the determined, hardworking spirit that he embodied. Today, we call it grit.

It also made one thing extremely clear to me: I wanted one of those diplomas for myself. I wanted to hang a bronze imprint of my own diploma from The Ohio State University in my own office one day. Up to that point, he was the only one in our family who had earned a college degree. Because of him, I was determined to be the second. Indirectly, he was passing on his grit to me.

It would be a while before I'd see it, but in those many days I spent with him, my grandfather was influencing the rest of my life. He was teaching me not to take shortcuts or cut corners. He was showing me the importance of thoroughly understanding how things work. He was demonstrating that if you're willing to put in the work, you're going to be okay. Again, grit.

Unfortunately, those lessons took a while to truly manifest in my life. As I grew into my teen years, my grandfather's influence on my life began to fade.

As I got older, I also got busier and more concerned with hanging out with my friends than spending time with my grandparents. My grandfather started to experience some health problems, and the Sunday dinners at my grandparents' house that had been a staple of my childhood became more and more infrequent. Slowly but surely, I began to drift. Without his influence, the discipline that was such a trademark characteristic of his life completely disappeared from mine.

I had just turned fourteen years old the first time I was arrested. (Yes, the first time—not the only time.) After the last day of eighth grade, I went with my friend George Brand to the Graceland Shopping Center in Columbus, Ohio. Before video games grew into what they are today, we had arcade game machines you pumped quarters into. Donkey Kong was a favorite. The Kroger grocery store in Graceland had a Donkey Kong machine inside, and I would watch George play for hours. He had it nearly mastered.

After playing Donkey Kong that day, somehow George and I were able to acquire a twelve-pack of beer, and we went behind a nearby bowling alley to drink it. We were having a great time right up until a police officer showed up. George and I were taken downtown and put in a jail cell in the early evening. My stepfather (who married my mom when I was ten) came and picked me up around midnight. To this day, I think the police waited until 11:00 p.m. to call my parents, just to make it sting that much more. I'm not sure which was harder—the car ride home with my stepfather or facing my mother when I walked into the house. The experience stuck with me, but it wasn't enough to keep me from doing it again.

By the time I got into high school, having as much fun as possible had become my sole purpose. Making sure I was present at the next party became my highest priority. The fear of missing out on a good time overrode any focus or potential I might have had in any other part of my life.

I did have some potential, especially when it came to sports. I could hit home runs in baseball, score goals in soccer, and throw a football better than most of my friends. I even taught myself how to kick sixty-yard field goals. (I know that last sounds fake, but it's true. I'll talk more about it later.)

The problem was, I didn't do any of this on actual sports teams. I didn't want to commit to the discipline of daily practice that could get in the way of my partying, so the structure that could have reentered my life through team sports stayed on the sideline. My athletic skills came out in random pickup games at the park where I tried to impress my friends or make them laugh. As always, my main focus wasn't on my future—it was on making sure I didn't miss out on the next opportunity for a good time.

Looking back, I do believe seeing my grandfather less during this time played a big role in my lack of discipline and some of the decisions I made. But my family history played a role, too. Growing up with divorced parents in the 1970s made you the exception, not the norm, and my parents split up when I was so young that I have no memory of it. For most of my childhood, I had no stable male figure in my life other than my grandfather. And when you come from a situation like that, you start doing things to get attention and to get people to like you.

That was me. I was lucky to have my grandfather's influence in my life, but I didn't have the steady, secure family situation at home that most of my friends had. My mom was busy trying to support us financially as a single parent, and she did the very best she could. She put me in amazing elementary and high schools, and she supported me in whatever I wanted to try. She gave me everything she possibly could have in the position she was in.

But there was only so much she could do for me as a single mom who had gotten pregnant with me as a teenager. I turned elsewhere for the attention and affirmation I didn't realize was missing at home.

I acted out. I made self-destructive decisions. I squandered my talent both in athletics and academics. If there was a school assignment that I didn't want to do because there was a party that night, I just wouldn't do it. If there was a test I decided I didn't care about, I'd get a D-minus, even though I was smart enough to get an A.

When I was sixteen, some of my friends and I got our hands on some old-school fake IDs that we used to hit the bars near Ohio State's campus. I became addicted to the experience. It was all I wanted to do. I was constantly looking for the next case of beer and a group of friends to share it with.

By my senior year of high school, I had accomplished basically nothing, and that was just fine with me. I consciously made it my goal as a senior to do as little work as possible while still graduating. What was the difference between a 1.9 GPA and a 3.7 GPA, as long as I got to be done with high school when it was over?

I followed through on my goal so well that on the second-to-last day of my senior year, I decided it would be a good idea to go to every teacher at Bishop Watterson High School and double-check that I had done enough to graduate, just to make sure. I had some threshold of embarrassment, and I didn't want to be that kid who walked up on stage, flipped open the fancy folder, and didn't see a diploma inside. The last thing in the world I wanted to do was go to summer school when I was supposed to be done with high school forever.

Most of my teachers told me I had done barely enough. I walked from classroom to classroom, hearing about the proud collection of C-minuses and D-pluses I'd assembled. Then I got to my home economics class, and the teacher told me I was failing.

Home ec? Seriously? I was no star student, but I'd managed to scrape together passing grades in chemistry, calculus, history, American literature, and all my other hard classes. How could I fail home ec?

That was the very question I asked my teacher, and she looked at me with total exasperation. "All I can tell you," she said, "is that there was one assignment I never received from you, and it's the reason you're failing. I did get one paper turned in with no name on it." She held the paper up to me. "Is it yours?"

Looking back, I don't know what I would have said if I had looked at the paper and seen someone else's handwriting. Would I have lied about it to avoid summer school? Would I have had the backbone to be honest and accept that I needed to do some actual work to earn my diploma? Could I have looked my teacher in the eye and claimed credit for work that wasn't mine?

Luckily for me, I didn't have to make that decision. I looked at my paper, and though there was no name on it, the handwriting was mine. I told my teacher, and thankfully, she believed me. She told me that with the paper, I'd done just enough to pass the class. No summer school for me. To this day, I can still feel the relief I had the moment I realized I had passed my senior year of high school. It's probably why I still triple-check everything, even now.

I'd achieved my goal of graduating while doing as little work as possible, but my last-minute brush with a failing grade in home economics emphasized how close I'd come to pushing it too far. I managed to walk across that stage and receive my diploma, but out of the 313 students who graduated from Bishop Watterson High School in Columbus, Ohio, that year, I ranked 312th.

And then, high school was over. All my friends were about to go off to college, and the parties I'd wrapped my life around would move on with them. I had no plan, no ambitions, no direction, no sense whatsoever of what I wanted to do with my life.

I'd applied to a few schools because that's what my friends were doing, but no one had any reason to accept me. Though my grandfather was an Ohio State graduate, I didn't have an "in" there, or anywhere else. I obviously didn't have the grades. I'd taken the ACT once, hungover on four hours of sleep, and I'd scored high enough that it wouldn't cause most colleges to turn me away but not high enough to impress anyone.

Even at that moment in my life, having gone through high school completely directionless, I still had one image in my mind that pulled on me like gravity: that Ohio State diploma hanging in my grandfather's office. I didn't know what I wanted to do for a career. I had no idea how I'd even make it through college after barely scraping by in high school. But I'd always had it in my mind that I was going to get a diploma from Ohio State like my grandfather. So, I decided I was going to try to get into The Ohio State University.

My grades were bad, but I wasn't naïve. I knew there was no way the university was going to accept me as a traditional student. I didn't even bother applying for the fall semester. I thought that maybe if I tried enrolling as a part-time student for the summer session, I'd be able to sneak in ahead of the crowd, and then maybe they'd let me in for the fall. I understood how the system worked. My grandfather's ingenuity and influence shone through me, though in a backward way that probably wouldn't have made him particularly proud.

I applied for the summer session, and they wait-listed me. My grades were so bad, I got wait-listed for summer school. Soon after, though, I found out that they were going to let me in. I had coasted my way through high school, then I had wiggled my way into Ohio State. In June 1988, barely two weeks since I'd graduated high school in less-than-stellar fashion, it was time for my first college class.

Unfortunately for me, getting accepted into college didn't guarantee any level of success in college whatsoever. When I started class the second week of June, I was completely unprepared. It was a total disaster. I failed to complete the summer session, and then in the fall, I was able to stick around long enough to hit a few tailgate parties at Ohio State football games. Before football season was over, I was dismissed from the university where my grandfather had earned his diploma.

I knew I'd have to tell my mom eventually, but I had become pretty detached from any family-related activities at that point. I would often go weeks without speaking to my mom. Just like in high school, I was too busy running around, doing my own thing, looking for the next party. I knew she wouldn't be happy that I was out of school, and I didn't tell her for weeks, maybe even months. And when I finally did tell her, I didn't mention that I had been kicked out. I told her I stopped going.

I had moved through most of my teen years completely focused on my own enjoyment in the moment. But at some point, you have to look at yourself in the mirror and recognize reality for what it is. I had barely scraped through high school. I had gotten kicked out of college. I had squandered my athletic talent and any academic potential I might have had. The friends I had once spent all my time partying with were growing up, and they were focused on their schoolwork. They were working toward making something of themselves.

I remember very vividly sitting in my bedroom at my mom's house completely directionless. I sat on the edge of my bed, looking around at the pictures of sports heroes and fighter jets plastered on my wall. I distinctly remember telling myself, "I gotta get it together, man."

I made my way down to the kitchen, and I did what any self-pitying, just-dismissed-from-college kid would do: I started making mac and cheese.

And as I watched the water boil, the phone rang.

CHAPTER 2

FOURTH AND LONG

THE VOICE ON the other end of the phone line belonged to a recruiter from the United States Navy. How he had gotten my number, I still don't know. Maybe I was on some kind of prospect list for kids who flunked out of college.

"Chris," he said, "what do you have planned for the future?"

He didn't need to say anything else. I had just failed to even make it to the end of football season at Ohio State. I had nothing going on, and I had no plans for the future whatsoever.

The recruiter came out to talk to me in person the next day. He gave me his pitch, but I had made up my mind before he even showed up at my house. I knew I needed to do something to get my life together.

I enlisted the very next day.

Boot camp was at Great Lakes Naval Station in northern Illinois, just south of the Wisconsin border. There were a hundred other men in my company, and of those hundred, around seventy were criminals, drug addicts, alcoholics, and others who had turned to the military because they had nothing going for them. I was lucky not to be a criminal or an addict, but I fell into the last group easily. The Navy felt like my last resort.

Somehow, despite my bad habits and lack of discipline, I got singled out fairly early as a leader. Maybe it's because I was athletic, or because I have a deep, loud voice. In any case, I became the recruit chief petty officer in boot camp—the leader of my company. I was in charge of making sure everyone stayed together, showed up on time, didn't get into any fights, and generally behaved themselves. All of those tasks were daily challenges.

I'd already experienced the reality that my actions had consequences when I was kicked out of Ohio State, and I was getting a lesson in that at boot camp as well. I was seeing firsthand that while I didn't have to follow the rules, there would be consequences if I didn't. I could screw around all I wanted, but I would have to pay a price.

I made the decision that boot camp was not the place to pay those consequences. We heard stories about other recruits who caused enough trouble to get sent back home and others who just quit. In both cases, the urban legend was that you would sit in a holding barracks for twelve weeks, waiting for the government to process you back to civilian life. Boot camp was only eight weeks. This seemed like a good time to follow the rules.

I was beginning to learn some measure of accountability, and those lessons extended beyond leading my company in boot camp.

My rating, or military job, was fire controlman. I still believe it is one of the cooler jobs in the Navy. To put it simply, I was the one who got to shoot the guns and missile weapon systems and learn how to fix them if something broke down. It was not something to mess with. There were real stakes if I didn't do my job right, and sometimes those stakes were people's lives.

I spent four years in the military. I never would have guessed it, but there was something about all of it that appealed to me. I liked the structure. I liked the accountability. It was something I hadn't experienced much growing up, and it brought with it a level of security and consistency that I'd been missing.

The United States Navy taught me a great deal about leadership, advanced electronics for weapons systems, and how to clean a bathroom to perfection. But one thing I still hadn't figured out was what I wanted to do with the rest of my life. I had grown, no doubt about it, but I was still directionless.

When I went home, I started aimlessly hanging out again. I didn't know what else to do.

My mom knew, though. Every time I found myself stuck as a young adult, she'd say the same thing: "Get yourself into school. Go learn something."

So, that's what I did. I enrolled at Columbus State Community College, and I discovered a new career path: being a paramedic. I had sort of stumbled my way into it, but here's the thing: I loved it.

For the first time in my life, I felt like I'd found something that I was truly passionate about. I loved everything about it. It was exciting. It was high stakes. And I got to experience the brand-new feeling of helping somebody when they couldn't help themselves. Helping others—that was something that would stick with me for the rest of my life.

I watched people who were struggling to breathe suddenly feel better after I gave them an oxygen mask. I got to see people respond to drugs we'd push through an IV. I experienced the impact I could have on someone who was hurting just by being there with them, showing them that they weren't alone. I knew very quickly that it was what I wanted to do.

Someone at school told me that if I went to a fire station and told them I was a paramedic in training, they'd let me ride along. That sounded amazing. So, I walked into a fire station for the Columbus Fire Department (CFD), and I was lucky enough to meet the right guy, Kevin Harr. I told him I was enrolled at Columbus State (which happened to be *the* place to learn to be a paramedic), and I asked if I could ride along. He agreed.

Kevin was great. He was shorter than most, and with his fantastic handlebar mustache, he looked like he could've been in a barbershop quartet. He was also a paramedic instructor, so he was engaged in my development. I rode with Kevin nearly every day that he worked for the next two years. I didn't have anything else going on besides school, so I had the time, and I loved it so much, I didn't want to do anything else anyway.

I finished at Columbus State, and I got a job for a small private ambulance service that worked jobs like Friday night high school football games and responding to overflow 9-1-1 calls when other medical vehicles were busy. The job paid only about $8.50 an hour, though. I knew if I was going to make a living as a paramedic, I needed to get hired on with a fire department.

Getting a job at a fire department as a paramedic was a three-step process, and I went into it believing that I was the best paramedic in the whole world. I *was* pretty good, but I didn't think I was only pretty good—I thought I was the best. I figured I'd go through the process and watch every fire department in the area line up to hire me.

The first step in the process was a written test, and it did nothing to curb my arrogance. I had always been good at retaining information, especially when it came to things I cared about, and I cared about this a lot. On the CFD test, I scored a 92, which was better than any score most of my paramedic and firefighter friends had ever seen.

"Dude," I was told several times, "you're in."

Next was the physical agility test, and I went into it feeling pretty full of myself. I considered myself an athlete, even though I hadn't played on a sports team since middle school. While I definitely could have done better, my performance wasn't going to keep anyone from hiring me.

Then came the last step in the process: the background investigation.

All the arrogance in the world couldn't keep my past from catching up with me. I knew they weren't going to find any atrocious crimes on my record; I hadn't done anything horrible. The problem was, I hadn't ever really done anything good, either, and the arrests in my early teenage years started to circle back.

Every job I'd ever had, I'd quit. I got kicked out of Ohio State. I had a ton of speeding tickets. Despite my honorable military service and my (limited) experience as an EMT, my record contained enough negatives to make any fire department pause.

After the background investigation, my name was put on a list. Candidates sit on that list for a while—sometimes as long as two years—waiting to receive an offer from CFD. I waited, and waited, and waited, but despite my high test scores and connections in the EMS community, I never got an offer.

Then I took Cincinnati's test, but the result was the same. I tested well, but then I got passed over. I took the test in Upper Arlington, Ohio, scored among the top ten applicants, and got passed over again. Over the course of about three years, I took tests, got put on lists, waited, and heard nothing. Over and over again; rinse and repeat.

Being a paramedic was the first thing in my life I had really, truly wanted to do. It was my first real passion. But the denials kept stacking up. Eventually, I had no choice but to acknowledge the obvious truth: I was never going to get hired by a fire department and therefore would be unable to make a living as a paramedic. I decided to move on with my life.

I was leaving one of the few things that had given me direction. I was back to square one, only worse because now I knew what it felt like to have something you cared about—a reason to get up in the morning—and then it was gone. I had lost what at the time felt like the only thing that had given my life any meaning or direction.

Around this time, I met a girl. I was immature. I had nothing going on in my life. I had almost no experience with any form of commitment. So, naturally, I decided it would be a good idea for us to get married. (Because that solves all of life's problems.)

Spoiler alert: it was not a good idea for us to get married.

I'm not going to spend a lot of time talking about our relationship in this book because there's not much good to say. Our marriage was a disaster from day one. By year three, I knew it was never going to work. In year four, we separated. We were officially divorced before our fifth anniversary.

I was not ready to be a husband. I was just looking for something to give my life some form of meaning. So, I asked, she agreed, and we got married. My dream of being a paramedic was gone, so we packed up and moved out of Columbus to Utica, Ohio, which was close to my wife's family.

Utica was a small farming community, only about forty-five minutes from Columbus, but to us, it represented exactly what we were looking for: the cheapest possible place to live. I had no career direction, and the only schooling I'd ever completed successfully was for a job I now knew I'd never have, so my money-making options were limited.

I worked a couple of different warehouse jobs in Columbus, which meant I drove forty-five minutes each way to pack boxes of random stuff. When I got tired of one job, I'd quit and find a different job, where I'd do basically the same thing, make basically the same money, and feel basically the same amount of miserable. The best job I found was mowing the grass at a local golf course for five dollars an hour, which I did mostly so I could golf for free.

I was disengaged from my work and from my life. I'd developed some leadership skills in the Navy, but I did nothing with it. I experienced passion for the first time as a paramedic, but that was gone, too. All my old drinking buddies from high school had moved on with their lives, gotten married, and found good jobs. Sometimes they'd go on vacations together and invite me to come along, but I could never go—seven dollars wasn't enough to pay for a vacation, and that's all I had in my bank account.

Everything was becoming a massive disappointment to me. It felt like my entire life was unraveling.

I had no idea where to turn.

And then, football saved my life.

CHAPTER 3

FORWARD PROGRESS

IN 1986, MY junior year in high school, Ohio State played against Alabama in the Kickoff Classic, the first game of the college football season. Both teams entered the season ranked in the top ten, and it was the biggest nonconference game Ohio State could have hoped for to start their season.

The game was close from start to finish. Alabama kicked two early field goals to take a 6-0 lead, and then Ohio State stormed back to lead 10-6 going into the fourth quarter. But Alabama scored a touchdown to jump back ahead by three and then added a field goal to lead by six going into Ohio State's final drive of the game. Jim Karsatos, Ohio State's quarterback, managed to drive them down the field, but his last-second pass to future Hall of Famer Cris Carter in the end zone was broken up, and Alabama held on to win, 16-10.

It was an exciting game, full of great plays by two great teams. But my takeaway didn't have anything to do with any of that.

My focus was on Pat O'Morrow, Ohio State's placekicker. He attempted three field goals in the game, and he missed two of them. Two field goals. Six points. Exactly the difference in the final score of the game.

I couldn't get it out of my head. If he had hit those field goals, we would have been tied. We could have won that game!

I had played soccer throughout most of my childhood and knew how to manipulate a ball with my feet, so I wondered how hard kicking field goals could be. How difficult was it to kick a little, weird-shaped brown ball between a pair of long yellow poles?

I decided I was going to find out. I went to the local Kmart, bought ten footballs, and started kicking. Right away, I learned the answer to my question: kicking footballs was *hard*.

At first, I was terrible. Nothing I kicked got more than a foot off the ground. But I'd spent my entire childhood kicking a soccer ball, so I knew I could do it. It was in me somewhere. (Again—grit.)

And one hot day near the end of the summer of 1987, it happened.

I kicked the ball and—BOOM.

I heard something that sounded like an explosion, and when I looked up, I couldn't see the ball. I looked up a little higher, and there it was, soaring what seemed like a mile in the air. Somehow, physically, I had figured it out. I had taught myself how to kick a football.

After that, kicking footballs became something I'd do for fun. When I was in high school, I'd go out and drill fifty-plus-yard field goals to impress my friends. After high school, when my friends were off in college or building their careers and families and I had absolutely nothing going on, which was often, I'd go find an empty football field and kick for hours at a time. It was something I could go back to, no matter what was happening (or not happening) in my life. Something I was good at. Something nobody could take away from me. Some people have yoga, some read multiple books a month, some bury themselves in corporate work. I kicked field goals. It became my safe place.

When I moved to Utica, I had absolutely nothing going on, as was typically the case. So, I did what I would always do: between my jobs at the warehouse and mowing golf course fairways, I'd go to the local high school football field and kick. I'd carry my bag to the football field, split the uprights, and smile with accomplishment.

One day while I was out practicing my placekicking, a man approached me. I knew who he was—Randy Felumlee, the head coach of Utica's high school football team. I had no idea why he would want to talk to me. Maybe it was to tell me to go home and stop trespassing on his football field.

Instead, he asked me a question that changed my life.

"Hey," he said. "You clearly know what you're doing out here. I coach the high school football team. Do you want to help out?"

I had never really considered coaching football before. But, like always, I had nothing else going on. "Sure," I said.

"Great," Coach Felumlee said. "Practice is every day at two thirty. Come on up, and we'll get you working with the team. We can pay you $2,500 for the season."

That may not sound like much money for several months of work, but I had never had 2,500 of anything before. I was getting offered $2,500 to be around football every day?

Sign me up.

I joined Coach Felumlee's staff as an assistant coach, but my main role was head coach of his junior high team. I was tasked with developing these young players and getting them prepared to work under Coach Felumlee when they reached high school. It was great for me because, for the first time in my life, I was accountable for the development of other people. Even better, it happened to be in an area I was developing a passion for: football.

I was in charge of practice every day. You might think that coaching a team of junior high kids would be relatively simple, but I learned pretty quickly that if I didn't go into practice with a solid plan, it was going to be complete chaos. I started developing a process for planning and time management. We would start at a specific time and end at a specific time. We would dedicate blocks of time to certain groups. I built a schedule that would help us move with a purpose, and I began learning to use resources (in this case, practice time and other coaches) efficiently.

I found an old storage box I had kept from the only other time I'd played football: eighth grade. Inside was a tiny ten-page playbook containing the entirety of the offensive system we ran when I was in middle school. It was perfect for the same age group of young men I was coaching. I combined that with the list of base plays that Coach Felumlee gave me, and suddenly I had a collection of football plays I needed to teach these middle school kids to run.

Suddenly, I'd gone from having nothing to identifying a very specific, real passion that I couldn't wait to pursue. A bunch of young people were depending on me to be their coach, and I actually cared. It was exciting, thrilling even, to dive into the playbook, dream up plans for practice, think about ways to put our best players in the best positions, and help the team win games.

I had a lot to learn, including the language of coaching. But even that excited me. I thought it was the coolest thing ever to be able to talk like a football coach. *"Power left waggle right forty-two sweep! Strong right forty-seven counter! Rocket mesh twenty-two blast!"* It was awesome. The more I learned, the better I got at teaching the kids I was working with. And the more I learned, the greater my hunger to learn more.

I'd sit at the kitchen table in the evening dreaming up plans to put our best players in positions to make plays. *If we're on the left hash, and I put the strength of the formation to the right, then put a guy in motion from left to right to overload the right side, the defense will shift all the way over to match up. But then, if I hide our best player on the left where no one expects him to get the ball, he's going to end up one-on-one with a defender, and our best player is going to win that match-up almost every time.*

It gave me goosebumps. I couldn't get enough of it. Every time I came up with a new concept, I couldn't wait to get up the next morning and install it in practice.

Football saved my life because it gave me a reason to get up in the morning.

I wasn't selling widgets. I wasn't going to a corporate job stapling papers on my desk just to set them on someone else's desk. I was doing something that I loved while also making a difference in the lives of these kids. We were playing a game. It was fun! At the same time, I got to help them develop as players and as people. It gave my life meaning. Somewhere in the middle of it all, it dawned on me that I was also teaching them about life.

Of course, the kids weren't the only ones who were developing as people. In coaching, I found a measure of accountability for myself that inspired me to be better than I had been. Going in, I hadn't expected how rewarding coaching was going to be, or how much I'd love teaching these kids a skill they didn't previously have, helping them implement it, and watching them succeed. Getting to be a part of that was amazing.

Coaching football awakened a passion in me. I didn't know exactly what or how, but I became fully convinced that I had a future somewhere within the sport of football. Somehow I *needed* to stay connected to this game.

The more time I spent around it, the more I realized how unique football was among the most popular American sports. In base-ball and softball, if you get a hit only 30 percent of the time at bat, that's above average, maybe even good enough to get into the Hall of Fame. You can play in the outfield and maybe get the ball hit to you a couple of times per game, or maybe you don't. In basketball, if you go three-for-seven from the floor, that's an okay day. In soccer, you might play for long stretches of time without ever coming near the ball.

Football is the only sport where, most of the time, you're lining up against the same person, over and over again, all game long. Your success or failure against that person on every single play can go a long way in determining whether your team wins or loses the game.

If you succeed, you've done your job. If you fail, you might find yourself in the dirt with a life decision to make: Are you going to get back up and keep going, or are you just going to lie there? Football forces you to get up. Lying there isn't an option. With every play you make, you must decide whether to fight harder than the previous play. Every twenty-five seconds, a life choice needs to be made.

The kids I coached had to make that decision about fifty times each junior high game. The person they lined up across was trying to demoralize them, remove their will, bury them, convince them that there's no reason to even get up.

As their coach, I had a job to tell them, "No matter what, get up. Make a choice. Decide that no matter how many times you get knocked down, you're always going to get back up."

And all this time, there I was, having been knocked down a thousand times by life and my own bad decisions, but I hadn't gotten up. Before football, my life had been unraveling around me, and I was doing nothing about it. I was losing and just lying there accepting it.

If I was going to teach the young men of Utica to get back up, I knew I had to start doing it for myself. I wasn't willing to give them empty words, challenges that I wasn't also willing to live up to. I had to get back up. At that point, I made my own decision to never ask anyone to do something that I wasn't willing to do myself.

I decided it was time to go back to college.

Even with all the goals I had abandoned, there was one I hadn't: I still wanted a diploma that said "Ohio State University" across the top. I wanted to be like my grandfather. I knew it wouldn't be an easy process. Ohio State wasn't likely to welcome me back with open arms after my first performance there, but I didn't care. No matter how difficult the challenge was—if I had to take remedial classes, start at a community college, or anything else—I was willing to do whatever it took to prove to Ohio State that they should give me another chance.

I was ready to put in the work. If I was going to teach kids to overcome adversity, I had to do it myself.

Ohio State had a satellite campus in Newark, Ohio, which was fairly close to Utica. I set up an appointment with an academic advisor to tell them what I wanted to do and, hopefully, figure out how to get the rest of my life started.

"Okay," the advisor said to me. "You're not going to get back into Ohio State right away. But if you want another chance, here's what you need to do. Central Ohio Technical College is right here on the same campus as Ohio State–Newark. Enroll there, get through a semester, and let's see how you do. If you handle that well, we can use it as a way to demonstrate to Ohio State that you're serious."

So, that's exactly what I did. The classes I enrolled in were general education classes like algebra, English, and psychology. But I took it seriously, like it was my job. Every assignment, every test, every single class I attended I approached with maximum effort. I wanted to be able to walk onto that football field knowing that I practiced what I preached.

And I did something I had never done before: I made it through the semester with straight A's.

After one successful semester at COTC, my academic advisor said, "Great work. Now go do another one." After two solid semesters, I got back into Ohio State as an undergrad freshman with zero earned credit hours trying to build a road into the Max M. Fisher College of Business.

Okay, so I technically got into Ohio State–*Newark*. I didn't care. I had redeemed my lack of drive, lack of effort, and lack of direction from my first attempt at college.

This time, I didn't stop at just getting in. I worked as hard as I possibly could. As I progressed, I was starting to see that I was building a road to success, starting to believe that I could actually do this. I could take a class and get an A. I could take multiple classes at the same time and get an A. I could take the *maximum* number of classes allowed by the university and get A's in all of them. Soon, I could see a pathway to graduation, and I believed I could get there.

Finally, at age 27, I was starting to grow up. I saw that I could make something of my life.

I started at Ohio State–Newark in January 1996. For that semester, I took as many credit hours as the university would allow. In each of the two summer sessions, I did the same thing. And by the end of the fall, even though it had only been a year, I had completed almost two full academic years of work. I was on a roll, and nothing was stopping me.

I continued like that all the way through my time in school. Except for a few months I took off to stay home with my daughter, Hanna, when she was born, I crammed as many classes as I could into each session. And at the beginning of 1999, I entered what would be my last semester of college.

I had worked hard, and I was incredibly proud of what I'd

accomplished in school. But I was also starting to think about what was going to come next. It was becoming clear to me that I was going to have to quit coaching and get a full-time job. The problem, though, was that I had no idea how to leave the game of football.

As I was nearing graduation, a teacher from Utica High School named Barbara Bruce reached out to me. Barbara was an outstanding teacher, someone the entire community of Utica respected, and (importantly) someone with a lot of influence over what happened in the school.

"You know, Chris," Barbara said to me, "if you would like to continue coaching football, we can make sure there's a teaching spot for you here. We'd love to keep you in Utica as part of our community."

I was interested right away. The possibility of working a job that would allow me to continue coaching sounded great. "That sounds great, Barbara," I said. "How much money would I make as a teacher?"

I'll never forget her answer. "Chris, we could start you at $19,500," she said quite proudly.

I knew at that moment that teaching wasn't going to work as a career for me. This was in 1999, and as I write this book twenty-five years later, teachers are still grossly underpaid for the incredible, valuable work they do. I knew that for me, I didn't have a passion to be in the classroom every day, and my desire to coach wasn't enough for me to be able to accept such a low salary.

"I'm sorry," I said. "I appreciate it, and I'd really love to continue coaching, but I need to be able to make more than $19,500."

That sealed it for me. I was leaving coaching.

None of that changed the fact that football saved my life. I graduated that spring knowing that my days of coaching alongside Coach Felumlee were over. But his impact on me turned my life around and is a huge part of why I finished college and why I am where I am today.

I didn't know what was next for me. But I knew one thing for sure: I didn't want to say goodbye to football. If I could possibly find a way, I wanted to stay connected to the game that saved my life.

CHAPTER 4

TAKING THE FIELD

I WASN'T READY to say goodbye to football. But I wasn't sure how to stay connected to it, either.

Becoming a teacher so I could coach football was out. I knew I didn't want to sell football equipment. I thought about trying to become a graduate assistant at the college level, but I quickly learned that graduate assistants don't get paid very much either—sometimes nothing. Plus, if I wanted to pursue a career in coaching, I knew I'd be moving around a lot, working for a few years and either taking a bigger job if I was successful or getting fired if I wasn't. I didn't want to move from small college town to small college town, having to rebuild a life at every stop. I also remembered some words of wisdom I'd heard from Mike Turk, who was head coach at Huntingdon College in Montgomery, Alabama: "There are two kinds of football coaches: ones who have been fired, and ones who haven't been but will be."

I couldn't imagine every two or three years having to tell my wife and children that our family would move again. That they'd have to leave their newly made friends behind and go find new ones. That they'd need to start over at a new school. And all the while, as a football coach, I'd have to work more than sixty hours per week, so I wouldn't be home to help much.

Then I thought about how many times I'd watched officials work while I was coaching. How many times I thought to myself, "I could do better than that guy, and I'd have a front-row seat to the game."

I'd already done some intramural officiating while I was studying at Ohio State–Newark. I saw it as more of a side hustle—a way to make some extra cash, and maybe something I could continue casually on the side after I graduated and got a real job. But I wondered whether it could be more. What if officiating was my way to stay connected to the game I loved?

I decided I'd give it a try.

In the state of Ohio, you have to obtain a license to officiate football. I was a bit ahead of the game there, though. My coaching side hustle in college had set me up for it. I found out where officiating classes were being held, spent six summer Saturdays in 1998 learning the basics of officiating, and took a test. I passed, earning my license. I was ready to get in the game.

And my first year was absolutely terrible. I may have known the rules, but actually managing the game is another skill set entirely.

If you ever want to learn to officiate a sport, start by officiating fifth graders in the rain. They'll do every crazy thing you can possibly think of. Looking back, I think some of those games were harder to work than games in the Big Ten and SEC.

You're not allowed to officiate high school varsity games in your first year as an official, though, so I had to take what I could get. Fifth and sixth graders, middle school games, maybe a high school junior varsity game here and there. Sometimes, I'd get paid only five dollars for a game.

I didn't care. This was what I wanted to do, and it wasn't about the money. I went at it full speed.

I knew going in I ultimately wanted to work my way up, so I worked every nonvarsity high school game I could. Junior varsity games. Freshman games. I officiated about four games per week over ten weeks. That's a lot of games in one season, and I enjoyed every one of them.

In my second year, I could see some of my hard work starting to pay off. I got picked up by a crew of guys who worked Friday night varsity games, and I worked the whole season with them. It was great experience to get under my belt, and it was my first time officiating under the lights with a crowd who really cared about what was happening. I got to soak in Americana at its finest—entire communities coming together to cheer on their team; the smell of hot dogs, brats, and shredded chicken sandwiches; and everyone standing and singing along with the national anthem. And I got the firsthand experience of looking at the guys next to me, understanding we're working together on the same team, and still thinking one inescapable thought: "I want to be better than that guy."

Football officiating is strange that way. It's a brotherhood, and we do everything we can to help each other become the best we can possibly be. But each of us still wants to be *the* best. I'll help you get better, but I'm going to do everything in my power to be better than you.

In my second year, I met Doug Murphy. Doug was a lifetime high school sports official, working across multiple sports including football, basketball, and softball. I got to be part of his varsity officiating crew for the next four years, and he taught me the world of officiating. He demonstrated how to carry yourself as an official, and (more than anything) he showed me how important relationships are to officiating, from the people who assign officials to games to the other officials on the field with you.

He also cared about me as a person. He'd call me on Wednesday to see how I was doing, even though we didn't have another game together until Saturday. He became a friend to me, and for the first time in my officiating journey, I got excited to be with the guys. It became less about the game itself and more about the relationships I'd formed and the time I got to spend with the others on our crew. I can remember sitting with Doug and others on our crew and laughing harder than I've ever laughed before. It's been over twenty-five years since then, and Doug still checks in on me and asks me what bowl game I have this year.

Football saved my life because it gave me strong bonds with other men that I'd never had before in my life.

I've phrased it this way already, and I'm going to do it again: it really is a brotherhood. It gave me real friends for the first time since I was in high school. It gave me a community. And unlike high school, it wasn't about parties. It was about working as a team to be the very best at something.

My ultimate goal in officiating was to get to the college level. I didn't care if it was the lowest-level junior college game out there, I wanted to be able to say I'd worked a college game. I'd reached the high school varsity level, and I'd even done well enough to earn some playoff assignments. But college football was calling.

It was time to start grinding. Grit.

I did everything I possibly could to break into the world of college football. I knew it wouldn't happen right away. Everyone told me to expect it to take at least five to ten years. But that didn't slow me down. I kept working hard at the high school level, and I went to every camp, clinic, meeting, and study group I could find.

I was doing all of this in the mid-1990s just as a new phenomenon called "the Internet" started to become widely adopted. There were no websites to look up, no message boards where I could ask questions, no social media where I could reach out to people who might be willing to help me. I did it the old-fashioned way with phone calls and letters.

It's amazing what people will tell you if you simply ask. I used to call the sports desk at *USA Today* to see if they had the phone numbers of some of the more well-known football officials working in college. They usually did, and to my surprise, they usually gave them to me. I called everyone I could, including Dave Parry, a big-time college football referee. Dave hosted a segment during televised football games called "You Make the Call," where the viewing audience would watch a football clip and then guess what happened during the play. I couldn't believe *USA Today* gave me his number, but when I talked to him, he was incredibly nice and helpful, giving me great guidance and names of people in my area whom I should connect with. He didn't have to do it, but he did. I've never forgotten his kindness.

The very first college officiating camp I attended was at Oberlin College in Ohio in 1999. I was fresh off my first year of varsity high school football, and while I was there, I met a guy named Jonathan Shelton. In the evenings, a bunch of us would sit around and talk through college football scenarios. Jonathan knew how to resolve every possible situation. There was no stumping him. Then, he'd play a "what-if" game with our group. What if the foul happens on fourth down? What if it happens during a punt? What if time runs out on the play when the foul is committed? What if there's a fumble with a change of possession before or after the foul?

Jonathan became a mentor to me, and that fall, he got me started working some small college junior varsity games on Monday nights. My first game was at Capital University in Bexley, Ohio, and even on that relatively small stage, I was scared to death. I wasn't sure if I could even walk onto the field. So, Jonathan essentially kicked me in the backside. I remember him telling me, "There's only one way to learn," and then pushing me out the locker room door like I was a kid who didn't want to go to the dentist.

It was the push I needed. It got me started on the path to get me to where I am now. I absolutely would not be here if it wasn't for Jonathan. He's still one of the best officials I've ever worked with, and when I'm lucky enough to get a postseason assignment, I still call him and thank him for that push he gave me twenty-five years ago.

After that game, I kept working and grinding. More camps. More clinics. Lots of conversations with more experienced officials. I worked hard for the next four years, officiating as many games as I could while balancing a full-time job in insurance.

I loved the work, but it was hard in those early days. I had a clear goal in mind—getting to the college varsity level—but so much of it felt outside of my control. I was constantly questioning myself. Was I doing things the right way? Was I in good standing with the people who could have an impact on my officiating career? Were there things I could be doing better? What if I was messing up and no one was telling me? It's so easy to question the uncontrollable external factors, but I never questioned the most important thing: my desire to succeed.

People would tell me to keep doing what I was doing, but I felt like I barely knew what I was doing.

The guidance and support of Jonathan Shelton and other people like him got me through. I kept working hard, kept doing everything the best way I knew how, hoping that it would all pay off eventually. I knew I had what it took.

So, I did the only thing I knew how to do: I kept grinding. I dedicated myself to preparation every week. I made sure that I was physically prepared to be on the field, and I constantly had my nose in the rule book. I was seeing my grandfather's determination to understand things show through in me. Slowly but surely, I could see myself getting better. The game was starting to slow down around me on the field, and I was seeing more of it in great focus.

In 2003, after five years of officiating at the high school level, I finally broke through.

I got the call. I was going to be part of a Division III officiating crew. Everything I'd been working for suddenly, in a moment, became real.

After everything I'd been through—and everything I'd put myself through—I had made it. I was going to be able to say I had officiated at the college level. I'd found something I cared about, worked hard at it, and accomplished my goal.

Now I just had to go do it.

My first game was on September 6, 2003. Thiel College at John Carroll University. I had never been so scared in my life.

From the moment I arrived, I could tell this was a different level of football. John Carroll University had a beautiful campus and wonderful athletic facilities, especially for a Division III school. Their stadium was named for Don Shula, one of their most famous alumni and a Hall of Fame NFL coach.

I'll never forget being in the locker room before the game. My eyes were as big as dish plates, and I'm sure it was obvious to just about everyone that I was terrified to be there. But David Jones, our crew's referee for the day, looked me in the eyes and with a calm and steady voice said, "Chris, nothing will happen out there today that we can't handle." I still haven't forgotten those words. They set the tone for me as an official as to how thoroughly I prepare every single week.

I managed to make my way onto the field, calmed a bit by David's reassurance, but still—if I'm honest—scared to death. My head was constantly on a swivel. I was terrified to call anything, but I was equally terrified to miss anything. I just didn't want to screw up.

The truth was, I knew the rules. I'd been preparing and working for that moment for the previous five years. But in the moment, when the lights are bright and you're on a bigger stage than you've ever been on before and it feels like the whole crowd is watching you to see if you're going to be the one to screw over their team, you don't feel as prepared as you actually are.

The game started, and I wanted nothing more than to quietly play my role and watch time tick off the clock. But the universe had a different plan. Just four plays into the game, I detected a problem. Thiel was preparing to punt on fourth down. The players were lined up in formation, and right as the ball was snapped back to the punter, an additional player from Thiel ran onto the field. I wasn't sure if he was the eleventh player (which is the correct number) or the twelfth (which is one too many). In either case, it was a problem for anyone to enter the field as the ball was being put into play. The gears in my brain felt like they'd been clogged with chewing gum, but I knew I'd seen something wrong. So, I did what any confident official should do when he notices a foul at the start of a play: I took my flag out of my belt, and I gently set it down next to my foot like it was a little puppy, trying to attract as little attention as possible.

That, of course, is exactly the opposite of what you should do as an official. Everybody—the players, the coaches, the crowd, the other officials—should know when you throw a flag, especially when it's before the play begins. That is the whole point of the yellow marker—to let people know you have identified a foul. But the only one who saw me throw that flag was me.

Thank goodness I had an experienced crew around me, with a referee who was a lot more confident than I was. After the punt play was over, once my brain caught up with me and I figured out why I had thrown the flag in the first place (it was an illegal substitution), the penalty was enforced, and the game went on. John Carroll went on to win easily, 42-0. I had survived my very first college football game.

Game by game, I became more comfortable in my role as a college football official. I became used to the environment, more easily able to function under the pressure of more fans and a faster-paced game. I became more and more proficient with my rules. And I began to realize something: At my age (33 at the time), with my experience, and in the kind of good physical condition I was in, I might not have to stop at Division III. I might be able to go after Division I.

Going into my third season officiating Division III football, I decided to give it a serious run.

If I was going to get into Division I, one target made the most obvious sense for me: the Mid-American Conference (MAC). The MAC was (and still is) a strong mid-major conference, and because I grew up, lived and worked in Ohio, it made sense for me geographically. The Big Ten was the top of the mountain, and getting to officiate there would be like a dream come true. But at the time, the MAC was a great option for me that seemed attainable for an official with my experience, and even if I never ended up making it any further than the MAC, I'd be able to say I'd worked Division I college football.

I continued doing the things an official does when they want to move up—going to camps, clinics, meetings, and making phone calls to anyone I could think of who might be willing to help me or point me in the right direction. Working at the college level gave me the confidence to flex a little more muscle with my networking.

One camp I went to was run by Dick Honig, one of the all-time officiating greats who worked as a referee in the Big Ten from 1983 to 2004. If you were an official in the Midwest and you had aspirations, Honig's camp was the mecca of officiating camps. All the big names and decision-makers were there. I had actually already gone to his camp for a couple of years, but this time, I reached out to Dick a couple of months before the camp and asked if I could come to his office in Ann Arbor, Michigan, to pick his brain. Dick, generous as ever, immediately agreed.

Dick owned an officiating uniform supply company called, of course, Honig's. We met in his spacious office, full of black-and-white zebra ornaments of all sizes, along with literally hundreds of pictures he'd taken with various crews he'd worked on across his decades as an official. We talked in his office for a while, and eventually, Dick stopped and said, "I have someone coming to fix the garage door at my house. Let's go for a car ride." We drove to his house, and after arriving, we continued to talk in his family room about officiating. But what Dick really wanted was to get to know me as a person.

Several weeks later, I came back for Dick's camp. I worked hard, just like I always did, and the day after I left, I got a phone call. I was getting assigned to work the spring exhibition game at Ohio State.

It was an unbelievable opportunity, and a great honor for me, especially as an official who still hadn't worked above the Division III level. As a graduate of Ohio State, I was (and still am) ineligible to work any of their regular season or bowl games to avoid any perception of favoritism or bias, so it would only be opportunities like this one that would allow me to interact with their football program. On top of all of that, this spring game happened to be after Ohio State's 2003 National Championship win. It was a big deal.

The game was one of my most memorable experiences as an official. The stadium was packed with over 90,000 fans as a result of the team's national title, and I got the full effect of being on a D-I football field. Many of my officiating friends told me there was a reason I got that assignment. I felt like I was on my way, and more than anything, I felt incredibly grateful to Dick Honig. Somehow I knew he had something to do with it.

Unfortunately, working that spring game didn't result in an invitation to join a D-I officiating crew. I worked that season in Division III, then the next season, and a few more after that. As I entered the spring of what would be my sixth year in D-III, I was beginning to doubt that I'd ever make it any further.

In the spring of 2009, I told myself I'd work one more year. If nothing came of it, that was okay with me. I'd officiated college football, which was always my goal, and no one could take that away from me. I'd go, work hard, give it my all for one more season, and if nothing happened, nothing happened.

Literally a month later, something happened.

In June 2009, my phone rang, and on the other end was Phil Barnes, the director of officiating in the Great Lakes Intercollegiate Athletic Conference (GLIAC).

My goal had been to get into the MAC, which was D-I. The GLIAC was D-II. Not what I was looking for, and still not something I wanted to do for the next ten years, even if it was a step up. I felt like I was in a position where I could turn it down if I wanted to because I had already been thinking of that year as my last. But it was still an opportunity, and I knew it was worth hearing Phil out at the very least.

"Chris," he said, "you've been doing such great work in Division III. We wanted to offer you an opportunity to come and join an officiating crew in our conference."

"Well, Phil, I'm going to be honest with you," I said. "I'm really enjoying my D-III schedule. But I am interested in becoming a referee. If I can be a referee, I'll come to the GLIAC, but if not, I'm not going to do it. I'll just finish things out in D-III."

Phil paused for a moment. "Okay," he said. "It's a deal."

"Okay, great." Feeling empowered with leverage, I said, "One more thing—I want a full schedule. Not just six games." It's common to be the new guy in a new conference and only get a handful of games.

"Not a problem at all," Phil said. "Glad to have you on board."

It wasn't Division I. But I had made it out of Division III, and now I had a new challenge to look forward to, possibly one that would help me get closer to the MAC. Also, it had always been a secondary goal of mine to be a referee. I had done it for a few games in D-III and once in a high school varsity game, but I was excited for the opportunity to get to do it full-time.

About a month later, the schedule for officials was released. I opened mine up, and I couldn't believe what I saw. I didn't have a full season. I didn't even have six games. I had five.

I did something unheard of in officiating circles: I called the supervisor right away and challenged him on my weak schedule. "Phil," I said, "we talked about this. You said I'd have a full season, no problem. What's the deal?"

"Listen, Chris," he said. I could hear in his voice that I was missing something, some important piece of information. "Obviously, you haven't heard yet. I don't like telling people this because we try to keep these things a surprise for you, but you're about to get another phone call. I'm not going to tell you who it's from. But you're going to want to answer it."

I'm not the smartest guy in the world. My brain told me to shut my mouth and say nothing but "thank you." Something told me that I was about to get the phone call every official waits for. So, I graciously thanked Phil and hung up.

Then I stared at the phone and waited for it to ring.

CHAPTER 5

THE BIGGEST STAGE

THE CALL WAS worth the wait.

A day or so after I got off the phone with Phil, my phone rang. It was Bob Waggoner, who was one of the leaders of the Collegiate Officiating Consortium (COC). The COC supervises the football officiating for the Missouri Valley, Mid-American, and Big Ten conferences. And Bob was calling to invite me in.

He invited me to join the COC for the upcoming season, primarily working in the MAC, with the possibility of even working a game or two in the Big Ten.

This was it. I couldn't believe it. I was in.

I worked a split schedule that season between the GLIAC, the MAC, and a couple of games in the Big Ten. My Big Ten assignments weren't glamorous—I was brought on as an alternate official (essentially a backup who likely wouldn't see the field) for games that would almost definitely be lopsided. Even if I had gotten into the game, there was very little damage I could have done.

I didn't care. I was officiating Division I college football. I didn't have to buy a ticket to get into the stadium. I got to put on my officiating uniform and stand out on the field. For my games in the MAC, I even got to work a full game a couple of times instead of standing ten feet off the sideline as the extra guy just in case of emergency. I was living my football dream.

The next season, I was invited to join the MAC for the entire season. I was an official, a full-time, no-doubt Division I official.

My first game of that season was Akron (from the MAC) visiting Penn State (Big Ten). I was the alternate official, but I didn't care. I was on the sideline for a game in a Big Ten stadium, and it was one to remember.

I'd grown up in Columbus going to Ohio State games in a stadium that could seat over 100,000 people. I'd heard the very loudest mobs in one of the most intimidating settings in college football. There was no topping it, or so I thought.

In the previous season, Penn State coach Joe Paterno had spent the year coaching from the booth up in the press box area due to an injury. The Akron game was his return to the sideline, and when he walked out of that tunnel onto the field, I felt the earth shake beneath my feet. I stood there, taking it in, absorbing all of it, and feeling incredibly grateful for where I was. I stored up that energy, determined to use it to drive me in the future.

Even now, I can remember that game like I'm standing right there in that stadium. My mind and heart were exactly where they needed to be. All of me was one thousand percent focused on what the next three hours would bring that day. I was fully present, fully engaged. Fully alive.

Starting in that 2009 season, I was a full-time Division I official. I worked in the MAC with a few games in the Big Ten here and there, and eventually, I transitioned into the Big Ten full-time. I wasn't allowed to officiate Ohio State games because I was a graduate of the school, but it didn't matter—I was at the top of the mountain. I got to be on the field, part of the spectacle of college football that had captured my attention and imagination for so much of my childhood. I had made it.

But it's funny how things that we work so long to achieve can disappear so quickly.

At the beginning of 2015, I called Bill Carollo, the Big Ten supervisor of officials, and shared with him that I had taken a job that required me to move from Columbus to Jackson, Mississippi. At the time, there was an unwritten but understood rule that to work in a conference, you had to live in a state that either housed a school in that conference or neighbored a state that did. Still, I respectfully requested that they retain me in the Big Ten. I'd already talked to my crew and prepared my referee, I had an excellent track record, and I'd shown that I was dedicated and committed.

Bill paused for a moment on the phone. "Chris," he said. "You're a great official. But I have to tell you, I think that's too far outside our geography, and I'm not comfortable with it."

I was crushed. I knew Bill was just doing what he believed was best for his conference. But it had taken me ten years to get where I was, and just like that, it was all over.

Bill stayed on the line, though. "Listen, Chris," he said. "We've been lucky to have you. Steve Shaw, the supervisor of the SEC, is a good friend of mine. Let me reach out to him and tell him that he needs to bring you in. You deserve to be on a college football field."

I already owed so much to Bill for where I was in my career. But the fact that he didn't simply wash his hands of me and move on—that he took time to help me when he didn't have to—spoke volumes about the kind of man he is. It's one of the reasons I still call Bill and thank him whenever I get a bowl game assignment at the end of the season.

Steve Shaw was the supervisor of officials in the SEC and Sun Belt conferences. The two conferences worked together similarly to the MAC and the Big Ten model, and living in Mississippi with Big Ten experience, I thought there was a good chance I might be able to get in with a recommendation from Bill.

That wasn't all. In 2014, the Big Ten was the first conference to utilize a new officiating position called the center judge on every crew it put on the field. I was one of the very first officials who made the switch to the position. The SEC had experimented with it in 2014 by implementing it in one of their eight crews, but in 2015, they were committing to it full-time with every crew. I knew they needed to hire at least eight center judges for the upcoming season, plus a few more for the Sun Belt. I was one of the only people in the world who had high-level college football experience at that position. I felt like it couldn't have been scripted better.

I set up a call with Steve, and I sat at my dining room table ready to go, freshly shaved, legal pad in front of me, three pens at the ready (just in case the first two didn't work). I called Steve.

"Hey, Chris," Steve said. "I'm so glad to meet you. Bill says nothing but the best things about you."

"Same here, Steve. Really glad to talk to you," I said.

"Listen," said Steve. "I just want to tell you that I've hired all my center judges for 2015. I'm afraid I don't have a spot for you this season."

I almost fell out of my chair. It felt like I was on an emotional roller coaster that I might never get off.

"But," said Steve, "what I want to do is invite you to our spring clinic in April at Mississippi State."

It was my second devastating phone call in a short period. But I pulled myself together long enough to say, "Yes, Steve, thanks so much. I would love to come to your clinic. I'll be there in April, and we'll move forward from there."

We hung up, and I was left with the feeling that I was out of football for good. Just as the dream was finally coming together for me, it was over. As a kid growing up in Columbus, I considered Big Ten football to be as good as it got. We made fun of those SEC guys who thought their football was somehow on a different level. And then, there I was, begging to get into the SEC, and I was getting shut out.

I felt like it was over.

I showed up at the spring clinic in April, back in the position I'd been in so many times: one of many unknown guys trying to break in with a marathon runner's bib safety-pinned to the back of my shirt. About a hundred other officials from various backgrounds were at the clinic, all trying to climb to the top of the mountain like I was. Except I had already climbed the mountain. To say I had an attitude about it would be an understatement.

I was assigned to head linesman, the position on the field I had before I'd moved to center judge. We were officiating a scrimmage, and each of us was in for a ten-play rotation, then back out, then back in again. I knew that if I ever actually had a chance of breaking into the conference, I needed to perform.

My turn arrived. On the first play, I was nervous and certainly more irritated that I needed to prove myself, again. The second play was better, but I officiated a little bit timidly. But at the end of the second play, I decided I wasn't going to leave that day without putting everything I had out on that field. I had officiated in the Big Ten. I'd been the best head linesman during my time in the MAC.

I was going to uncork it on these guys.

And I did. I worked the next eight plays like a demon. I had people walking up to me saying, "Damn. You're good."

And I'd look them right in the eye and say, "I know." (I'm not shy sometimes.)

I'd go in and report a foul at the end of a play—"holding on the offense, number 72, ten-yard penalty from the previous spot, and we are going to replay second down"—and the referee would look at me and say, "Wow. No one has ever given me that information so completely and succinctly before. That's fantastic."

And again, I'd reply, "I know. That's how everybody should give you the information."

I wasn't going to win any awards for humility. But I believed I was the best guy on the field, and I wasn't afraid to show it in my work and let everyone see it. I never said it out loud. I let the work do the talking for me. I worked it that way every time I was in the game. I hadn't worked as hard as I had for the last ten years for someone to tell me I wasn't good enough. I'd done bowl games and conference championship games, and I knew I deserved to be there.

When the scrimmage was over, an SEC official who was there observing approached me. "You're really good," he said, "the best we've ever seen at this camp. I'm going to recommend that we hire you."

Awesome, I thought. I'm in.

I was not in.

I got an email congratulating me on a great camp, but no job offer. A few months later, I was invited to come to the summer clinic at Arkansas to work some more and discuss what the upcoming season might look like for me. I went to the clinic, worked just as hard as I had in the spring, and waited to hear my fate.

The news wasn't what I had hoped for. I was being offered a position, but only as a supplemental official. Basically, I was going to be an extra guy floating around. I wasn't going to be on a crew. I'd have no consistency from week to week on who I was working with, no guarantee of work on any given week at all. It was better than nothing, but it was still several steps backward for me compared with where I'd been and where I felt like I deserved to be.

Steve Shaw, to his credit, gave me a full schedule of supplemental games that season. I was on a different crew every game, and for some games, I was the alternate and never got on the field. I worked a mix of Sun Belt and SEC games, and I was still disappointed about being passed over for a full-time spot with my experience. But it was better than being out of football entirely.

The next year, I went through the same process again. I was invited to come back to the spring clinic, and then the summer clinic, to work more scrimmages and be evaluated again. I was in the deep end of the grinding pool. I showed up with the same passion and intensity as the previous year and walked away knowing that I'd given absolutely everything I had. If this was the end of the road for me, it wasn't going to be because I didn't give maximum effort. And I received good feedback from everyone, including Steve, who was at the summer clinic in person.

A couple of months later, the crew assignments for the upcoming season were released. I was nervous but excited. I thought I had a real chance at being put on an SEC crew. And I *knew* I deserved to be on an SEC crew.

I looked at page one. The SEC crew assignments. I scanned the page, looking carefully across each of the eight crews, checking to see who was listed as center judge, and then checking the other positions, just in case. Then I double-checked to make sure I hadn't missed anything.

My name was nowhere to be found.

I flipped the page with the Sun Belt Conference assignments. And there I was, listed on one of the crews as a center judge.

I was on a crew. It was better than being out of football entirely. I was in the Sun Belt, not the SEC. It would have been like being put back into the MAC after working in the Big Ten. I didn't understand it. But it was pretty clear there was nothing I could do about it except what I'd been doing my entire career: go out and be the best damn center judge the Sun Belt Conference had ever seen.

I worked that season with the same passion and intensity that I'd brought to each of those spring and summer officiating camps. I was determined to demonstrate that I was good enough to be in the SEC and that, with all due respect, keeping me out of the conference was completely, unequivocally a mistake. I studied, prepared, and performed to the absolute best of my ability in the Sun Belt that season.

The next year, in 2017, I opened the crew assignments and saw my name listed as center judge on an SEC crew.

I had climbed to the top of the mountain, fallen off, and then, two full seasons later, made it to the top again.

What I'd soon understand, however, was that being in the SEC wasn't like being back in the Big Ten. I was on another mountain now.

Officiating in the SEC is on a completely different level. During my time in the Big Ten, I saw a couple of good teams, which led to high-profile matchups with giant, raucous crowds. But the Big Ten also had plenty of matchups between teams in the bottom half of the standings, and if I'm honest, the atmosphere at many of those games felt more like the high school games I'd officiated. The crowds were small, the energy was low, and while it didn't stop our crew from giving our absolute best, the stakes just weren't as high.

In the SEC, people show up at a game between the two worst teams in the entire conference and act like it's the National Championship game. They camp out at the stadium starting on Thursday before the game, and by the time the game starts, they've been in full-on party mode for days.

On top of that, there's no such thing as a bad venue or college town in the SEC. Every single spot has something to offer. My wife, Anna, whom I married in 2020, loves to go with me to Kentucky. We see the horse country on the way and often enjoy a bourbon tour on Sunday after the game. Vanderbilt is great because I know I'm going to get to listen to some good music while in Nashville. Georgia is consistently one of the loudest stadiums I've ever worked in. The party environment is palpable at both Ole Miss and LSU. Neyland Stadium at Tennessee gives me the same vibes that I got from Ohio State games as a kid, and when Tennessee is rolling, it's as loud as anywhere. "Sandstorm" at South Carolina is one of the best opening kickoff traditions in the country, and I'm lucky enough to stand right in the middle of the field with the ball at the start of the game, absorbing all that energy from the crowd. Missouri has seen their football program improve, and the student body and their fan base is responding with great enthusiasm. Florida is absolutely historic; you know you're in a special place whenever you walk on the field. Lots of Heisman Trophies and National Championships have come through Gainesville. The eagle soaring through the stadium at Auburn never gets old. Arkansas has one of the nicest stadiums in the conference with an incredibly passionate fan base. The cowbells at Mississippi State are something you won't experience anywhere else in college football. Kyle Field at Texas A&M is always full, the crowd chants through the entire game, and they have the best military flyovers. Alabama spent many years as the pinnacle of college football, and even now that Coach Saban has retired, its place in the sport is legendary. In late September 2024, we worked the third home game of the season for Texas in their first year with the SEC, and they had over 102,000 people in attendance. There was a lot of fireworks, smoke, cannon shots, intricate light shows, majorettes twirling flaming batons, and (of course) their famous mascot, Bevo. They put on a solid show. And I haven't been to Oklahoma yet, but I am anxious to see that chuckwagon race across the field.

Based on my experience, when people say SEC football is on another level, they're not wrong. Their motto—"It just means more"—is truly fitting.

I'll always remember my very first game in the SEC. It was during my time as a supplemental official during the 2015 season. I was also finishing out my appointment as president of the Ohio Association of Football Officials at the time. Earlier that year, Toledo's head coach, Matt Campbell, had been the guest speaker at the association's annual banquet. I had no connection to him other than being in the same room as him while he spoke to our officiating group. During pregame warmups, while some members of each team were out on the field, Coach Campbell saw me standing on the fifty-yard line. He made a beeline in my direction, and he gave me an enormous hug right in the middle of the field.

I was extremely flattered by Coach Campbell's gesture, but it wasn't exactly the image I wanted to give to others. Working the game in a fair and impartial manner to both sides is the foundation of everything I do on the field.

Toledo was a three-touchdown underdog in the game, but it was incredibly close the entire way. It came down to a final drive by Arkansas in the fourth quarter, three minutes left, Toledo leading 16-10. Arkansas ran the ball to the Toledo one-yard line, setting Arkansas up for what should have been the go-ahead touchdown. But on that play, from my center judge position, I observed Arkansas' outstanding tight end Hunter Henry tackle a Toledo defender who was coming through the line of scrimmage right where the running back was receiving the football.

The last thing I wanted was to be involved in a foul that would impact the game at such a critical time. But this was one of the easiest, most obvious holding calls I'd ever had. Even my evaluator—the person who grades every play of the game—wrote in his report, "May all your fouls be this easy and obvious!" I threw the flag and called the penalty, and Arkansas was unable to get the ball into the end zone. I can still clearly see the image in my head of Hunter Henry sitting on the ground holding his head with both of his hands. He knew what he had done. Arkansas later managed to force Toledo into a safety and had a last-second chance to win the game with a pass to the end zone, but they couldn't convert. Toledo went on to win, 16-12.

This game was my first time experiencing the energy and passion of the SEC as an official, and it reinforced two principles that will always be true for me. First, on the last play of a tie ball game, I don't want the play coming to me. I don't want to be the one to decide whether the guy caught the ball or not, whether he was inbounds or not, whether there was pass interference or holding or anything else that would affect the outcome of the play. And second—and more importantly—if there is a foul that impacts the outcome of a play, it's my job to call it, and I always will.

I'm now entering my eighth season on an SEC crew, and my tenth overall working games for the conference. With each year of officiating, you know that the clock is ticking on the amount of time you have left. It's demanding on your body, it's demanding on your schedule, and every year it takes a little more time and effort to prepare in the ways needed to achieve the highest levels of success.

But I know this: I will give this game everything I have for however many years I have left. I officiate football because I love it, and when it's time to walk away, I won't leave wishing I'd done anything better, worked harder, or prepared more. Every time I come out of the locker room, I am one hundred percent ready to go to work.

My journey has taken me in all directions, and it hasn't been easy (some of which was my own doing). But it got me to where

I am: officiating college football at its absolute highest level. It *is* a dream job. And for as long as I'm doing it, I won't take it for granted.

CHAPTER 6

OFFICIATING FAQ

WHEN PEOPLE LEARN that I officiate college football, they usually have lots of questions for me. I get it. It's an unusual job, and before I was doing it, I would have had a lot of questions, too.

So, I want to take this chapter to share answers to some of the questions I get most often as an official. Think of it as a peek behind the officiating curtain. Who knows—maybe you'll get some of your own questions answered, too.

What was Nick Saban like?

You'd be surprised how often I get this question, and now that he's retired, I feel that I can talk about it openly.

One thing I appreciated about Coach Saban was that whenever I worked his practices, he would meet with us to discuss the practice schedule and where he was focused on developing the team. He wanted us to watch details like alignment on punts, players getting set after going in motion before the snap, defensive back technique, etc. He genuinely wanted us to tell him if an adjustment needed to be made. I've worked several practices and scrimmages as an official, and few head coaches interacted with us as thoughtfully as he did.

It's no secret that on the field, Coach Saban was about as intense as they come. But during the many Alabama games I worked, it was rare that we ever had much of an issue with him. It seemed like he knew that his time was better spent with his players and coaching staff and that yelling at us was generally a waste of energy.

Now, don't get me wrong. I've worked enough Alabama games with Coach Saban to know that he was never shy about giving an opinion. A few times when I was on the sideline after a score during a media timeout, I'd notice him approaching me. (Trust me, I never sought him out.) My first thought in these situations was, "Uh oh, here comes Coach. He's probably right about something." And if he did speak to me, he usually was.

In those situations with any coach—but especially with someone as experienced as Coach Saban—the best thing you can do is listen and keep your mouth closed. It can make the three-minute SEC media timeouts feel like three hours. But I've come to learn that the coaches are not interested in hearing about your view of the situation because they know you aren't going to change the call. They just want to tell you how unhappy they are with your ruling.

Who is the worst coach you've ever worked with?

This is a very common question, but I would never call out a coach for being the worst. Sure, some coaches are easier to work with than others, but the world coaches operate in is nearly impossible for the rest of us to understand.

Coaches are hypercompetitive at a level that's foreign to the rest of us, and they are in a pressure cooker week in and week out. Imagine working eighty hours per week with the expectation of bringing in a top recruiting class, leaning on a bunch of 18- to 21-year-old athletes to make you successful, dealing with your fanbase's expectations that you win the conference and qualify for the College Football Playoff, all while working to ensure your school has enough NIL (name, image, likeness) dollars to attract the talent you need in the first place.

It's a lot of pressure, and different people respond to that pressure in different ways. When I have a difficult interaction with a coach, I try to remind myself of everything they're dealing with, offer them a bit of grace, and move on.

How long have you been officiating?

In 2024, I celebrated twenty-six years of officiating, dating back to my first junior high game in 1998. It's been a long time, and yet it went by so fast. Officials get only so many games in a season, and like most football fans, we officials start the countdown to the next season as soon as the last one is played.

Over the past couple of years, I've noticed something interesting. As I get older, some of the coaches get younger. Some of the head coaches in Divisions II and III, as well as some assistants in Division I, are in their mid- to late twenties or early thirties. Sometimes when they want to argue with me about a holding call, I have to take a breath and remember that I have been officiating games, studying the rules, and watching film for longer than they have been alive. Which brings us to the next question . . .

Do you aspire to get into the NFL?

For me, the NFL is a totally different game. On Sundays, after I get done with my SEC assignment, I may turn on an NFL game on TV, but that is mostly just for the sound. I am typically busy going through my game film from the night before several times.

Historically, the NFL had many officials with the same last name because their grandfather, father, uncle, or brother was already in the league. I never had that advantage. These days, the NFL has been very transparent about wanting to hire a more diverse pool of officials. I have zero problems with this and applaud the league for its transparency on it and for following through with it. My background doesn't check any diversity boxes either.

In the end, I always tell people that getting into the NFL is like winning the Powerball. You can't plan on it. One day it just happens, and you're not really sure why someone gets picked and someone else doesn't. I spend my time thoroughly enjoying the SEC and not wishing I was somewhere else.

Does it bother you when a coach screams at you?

It has never bothered me. I work extremely hard during the week to be comfortable with the challenges I will face on game day. Usually when a coach yells at me, I know that they are coming from a place of simply wanting things to go their team's way, which I can appreciate. It also comes from a place where they don't know the rules as well as I do, so their argument is typically invalid. This also ties back into the previous question of how long I've been officiating. I have well exceeded the 25,000-hour mark of practice, preparation, and game experience. All of the exposure to the game is a great insulator to those who want to argue. The only way it would bother me is if they were right about something, and that is rare.

What school do you work for?

We don't work for a school. All officials are 1099 subcontractors for the conference. We go where the conference tells us to go.

Which school is your favorite to visit?

As I mentioned in the previous chapter, every single SEC school is a wonderful place to travel. They each have their charms and quirks, and more than anything, they're all incredibly passionate about college football. I don't have a favorite place to go because I love wherever I get to go every single week. The passion that runs through the SEC makes you feel like you are working a bowl game every week. Even when we are working a game where both teams have losing records, there are still 65,000 fans cheering loudly.

Do you work with the same crew every week?

For the most part, yes. We have assigned crews for the entire season. This is helpful to build relationships, rapport, trust, and chemistry on the field (I'll talk a bit more about this in the next chapter).

There are some exceptions to this, though:

- You can't work a game that involves a school with which you have a business relationship. For example, we have several officials who provide business services to certain schools, and those officials declare such connections so that none of those schools appear on their schedule.

- You can't work a game that involves a school you graduated from, attended, or have a business relationship with. For example, the umpire on my crew played football at Alabama, so when we're assigned an Alabama game, he gets switched out.

When one of these situations comes up, the affected official is switched out with an official from another crew, and we move forward as normal.

This is slightly different at the beginning of the season, too. For most of the season, SEC teams are playing each other, meaning that most weeks, there will be eight games total (because there are sixteen teams in the SEC). But for the first three weeks of the season, teams play nonconference games. This dramatically increases the number of games that involve SEC teams, and it means that to get all of those games covered, we often have to mix crews up using officials from the SEC, the Sun Belt, and sometimes even a few guys from Division II conferences.

Is your travel paid for?

Nope. We're paid a flat fee for each game. We pay for our own transportation, meals, and hotel when we travel to games. This can get expensive quickly since many of our games are in smaller college towns where hotels make a large percentage of their income for the year during the six or seven weekends when home football games are scheduled and therefore their prices for those days go up significantly.

Remember, this is not a full-time job for us. No one is getting rich from being a college football official. Depending on expenses and tax situations, sometimes breaking even at the end of the year is a legitimate possibility.

What's it like to deal with college football fans?

It's all part of the job. But during the game, it doesn't even register. I'm so focused on the game action that the stadium could be empty and I wouldn't realize it.

I always say that after the game, half the stadium thinks it's your fault that their team lost, and the other half thinks you were trying to get their team to lose. From kickoff until the end of the game, if you're looking for a friend, you'd better have brought one with you because no one in the crowd is your friend, the teams aren't your friends, and neither are any of the coaches. It's you and your crewmates on an island, and the only way off is to perform at a high level.

Outside of that, though, we don't deal with any fans in the heat of the moment during the game. It's not a problem. They're interested in the work we do, and when they're not actively watching their favorite team get called for a (probably legitimate) holding foul, they understand what a difficult job we have. I enjoy the conversations I get to have with fans outside of game day, and I recognize that without them, I wouldn't get to do this amazing job that I love.

What are your interactions like with players on the field?

For about six seconds, the players will give everything they have to bury their opponent into the ground. Every single one of them will be in full-on beast mode, determined to physically punish anyone who gets in the way of them doing their job to help their team win.

And then, as soon as the whistle blows, they'll get up, nicely ask me a question, and almost always say "please" and "thank you." They might get frustrated when they don't agree with a call, but for the most part, they communicate respectfully and just want the game to be played fairly.

We try to do the same for them. We'll talk to players frequently if we believe they are repeating an action that's on the edge of being a foul, and if we see someone whose temper is running hot, we try to talk them out of making a bad decision. We would much rather proactively talk to a player and prevent a foul from occurring. Talking to players during the game is one of the more common and powerful officiating actions we employ.

I believe that's one of the hallmarks of a good official on the field, and it extends to leadership off the field as well. Good officials help someone before they get too far into the deep end of the pool and make a decision they're going to regret.

Do you ever interact with players or coaches off the field?

Short answer: no! There is no good reason to, and nothing good will come from it. All it takes is one picture of me with a player or coach on a random Tuesday night out somewhere in public, and I'd never be able to work at their school again. There would always be a perceived bias by the public. There's just too much risk involved.

How and when do you find out which games you're officiating?

Sometime in mid-July, we find out our assignments for the first four or five games of the season so we can make travel arrangements for the month of September. After that, once the season starts, we get our game assignments as the season progresses. Generally, I know my schedule about four weeks out at any given time, but no further than that.

There's a good reason for this. Imagine this: A situation happens during a week-five game at State University, and even though the officials did a great job and the game was free from error, State U questions why one particular ruling didn't go their way. Later in the season, that same officiating crew is due to work another State U game—a big rivalry game. Because the schedule is kept confidential, it's easy for the officiating supervisor to move that officiating crew to a different game, eliminating any chance that State U would be predisposed to question the officials' rulings during the game. The officiating supervisor can make the adjustment that's in everyone's best interest, and nobody would ever know it was an issue in the first place.

Are officials allowed to be fans of a college football team?

We're allowed to be a fan of anything we wish, but it's a bit unusual. Over time, officials become wired to watch a football game from an unbiased, technical perspective. We watch the officials more than we watch the players. We watch the clock inside the last two minutes of each half and think about when it needs to start in conjunction with the next play. It's great reinforcement for us. When we watch games together, we always talk one or two plays ahead about hypothetical scenarios. We just interact with the game differently, and it doesn't leave much room to watch the way a fan would watch. I also compare it to the old episode of *I Love Lucy* when Lucy and her friend Ethel are excited to get jobs at a chocolate candy factory. They get behind wrapping candy from the conveyor belt and start force-feeding themselves the chocolate treats in an attempt to catch up, ultimately making themselves sick. Similarly, we are so involved in football as a job that watching it for fun as a fan doesn't rank high on the list.

I can tell you this: I graduated from Ohio State, and I grew up watching Ohio State football. I know that Ryan Day is their head coach. But as I write this, I couldn't tell you the name of a single player on their roster. I just don't have an interest or need to watch it as a fan. (Ok, I will admit that I watched the 2025 CFP National Championship Game when they beat Notre Dame with some interest.)

Who decides when a new rule gets added?

Here's something most people don't know: officials have very little say in what rules get added, changed, or taken away. The rules committee comprises coaches and athletics representatives from a diverse group of schools. One official acts as a consultant, guiding the committee on how the current and proposed rule changes are adjudicated on the field, but officials don't make the rules.

It sometimes makes me laugh a bit on the field when a coach complains about a rule because his peers are the ones who thought it was a good idea to put it in the rule book in the first place!

How do instant replays work?

Replays happen when there is enough uncertainty as to whether the call made on the field was the correct call. It is an entirely different universe of officiating. You can take any play, and if you slow it down enough and look at it from the right angle, you can make it into practically anything you want. The initial instruction is to watch the play at real speed to determine if there is a suspected issue. When an issue is detected, they dig deeper. So, a TV commentator will say, "They review every play." The truth is they *look* at every play to see if it needs to be reviewed. There is a difference. If a team runs a super-fast offense, we may not even get the chance.

Sometimes, only three cameras are present at the game, and that's all the possible angles a replay official has. Other times, literally thirty-seven cameras are present, especially if it's a big bowl or championship game. Here's a secret about replay, though: the replay official is completely at the mercy of the producer in the TV truck as to what angles of the play they are and are not able to review. Another angle might exist out there somewhere that becomes available after the review ruling is announced and it offers the perfect view of the play, and they may even opt to show that angle on TV after the review announcement, but the replay official can only use what they're given in the very limited time they have to review a play.

In some ways, though, that's not the worst thing in the world. A human brain can only digest so many views at once. It can easily become technology overload, too much information to process at once. Replay officials are under an unofficial constraint of ninety seconds. It's not a hard and fast rule, but if a review takes more than a minute and a half, it starts to feel like it's taking forever. They don't want to be the ones responsible for ruining the pace of the game, so there's an urgency to expedite the process as much as possible.

Replay exists to help us make sure we get as many calls right as possible, but it's not perfect. It's limited by technology, time constraints, and the fact that the people using the technology are still human beings.

Do "makeup calls" exist?

They absolutely do not exist, and it's poor judgment for a commentator to claim otherwise. I have no interest in awarding a team a "makeup call" after a call they didn't like. There's just too much accountability for our actions on every single play.

Every call is judged on its own merit. Every single move we make is constantly being evaluated by an officiating supervisor. If an official starts making up calls in a game, it will be their last game.

We get graded and judged on the number of correct calls, missed calls, and incorrect calls we make. These are actual categories on the grade sheet I receive after every game, along with a few other more technical ones. If I call a foul that isn't there, that counts against me. If I decide not to call a foul that *is* there, that counts against me. The only reason I throw my flag on a foul is if I believe it occurs, and the only reason I keep my flag in my pocket is if I don't detect a foul.

If the system ever allowed for an official to take matters into his or her own hands, all trust in the integrity of the game could come crashing down. None of us are willing to let that happen.

Do you have any embarrassing moments you want to share?

Here is something very few people know. It was November 15, 2014, and our Big Ten crew was working at the University of

Maryland on a gorgeous fall day as they played the 15th-ranked Michigan State Spartans.

Before a game, it is common for officials to warm up before running around the football field for over three hours. We do all sorts of things in the locker room to get our bodies activated: push-ups, jumping jacks, exercise bike, and various forms of stretching.

At Maryland, our locker room was right next to the football team's weight room. The weight room was empty, so it was a great spot for me to get energized. At that point in my life, I was doing a lot of CrossFit, and I would commonly use something called a slam ball (think of it as an old-school medicine ball). It weighs ten, fifteen, or twenty pounds, and I would often do an exercise that involved holding the ball over my head, slamming it to the ground, picking it up, raising it over my head, and slamming it down again as many times as I could within a certain time limit.

So, when I saw several slam balls in the weight room, I got excited. I thought it would be a great way to loosen up and get my heart pumping in a short amount of time. Without paying too much attention, I randomly picked up a ball, hoisted it over my head, and slammed it to the ground. What I didn't know was that this slam ball bounced. It hit the ground and, with equal velocity, rocketed straight back up, hit me square on the chin, and knocked me out. I'm not exactly sure for how long—thirty, sixty or ninety seconds—but I lay sprawled out on the weight room floor. When I regained consciousness, I looked around to see if anyone had seen me being an idiot. Thankfully, the weight room was still empty. I collected myself and went on to work one of the smoothest games I've ever had.

Have you ever made a bad call that still haunts you?

My record as an official is fairly solid. Typically, I finish in the top third of officials at my position. Last season, I officiated 1,872 snaps, and I was wrong on two of them. I work hard at being decisive at the right time, making the best call I know how to make and moving on.

But there's one call that will eat away at me forever.

It was November 13, 2021. New Mexico State was visiting Tuscaloosa to play Alabama. New Mexico State had the ball, and on a play where they ran the ball up the middle, I saw an Alabama defender reach out toward the ball carrier. In the next second, I saw the ball carrier's head and shoulders snap backward as his feet continued to move forward. I threw my flag. Huge face mask foul.

I walked over to my referee to report what I had seen so he could announce the call to the stadium, but something wasn't sitting right with me. I've always had a rule about face mask fouls: don't call it unless you can see the fingers in the cage of the face mask twisting and pulling. I hadn't seen that, but with the way the running back's head and shoulders snapped backward, what else could it have been?

"What have you got?" my referee asked me.

"Uh, face mask on the defense, number 92," I said, without an ounce of conviction.

He looked at me. "Are you sure?" He could tell something was off.

"No," I said. "But that's what I am going with."

"Okay," he said. And he announced the call to the stadium.

As he was announcing it—literally as the words were coming out of his mouth—I heard thunderous boos from the crowd as they watched the big board in the stadium where they were showing a replay at a different angle. And right there, clear as day, was the defender grabbing the inside of the running back's *shoulder pads* and pulling him to the ground. A completely legal play that I had just awarded with a fifteen-yard penalty.

The stadium erupted in boos. I stood there, taking all of it, knowing that I deserved every last bit because I had broken my own rule. I had called a face mask without seeing the defender's fingers inside the face mask, and I was one thousand percent wrong. It wasn't even close. Every single person in the stadium could see it.

Of course, one of the people in the stadium was Coach Nick Saban, and during a TV timeout, he wanted to make sure I knew that he knew how wrong I was. "Coach, you're absolutely right," I said. "I got it wrong." All I could do was be accountable. He looked at me with the angriest expression I've ever seen, and then he turned and walked away.

Thankfully, my call didn't influence the game one bit. Alabama won 59-3. But that call still eats away at me because I knew better. That's why we work as hard as we do at it. The slightest mistake will eat at you for the rest of your career.

But I'll tell you one thing, you won't catch me calling that penalty anytime soon unless I'm positive I've seen fingers inside the cage of a face mask.

How dangerous is officiating? Do you ever get injured?

I got run over once or twice when I worked on the sideline early in my officiating career, and I've learned how to properly stay out of the way since then. But sometimes accidents still happen. You're in the middle of a game featuring big, strong athletes flying around the field at top speed. It's a dangerous position to be in.

On November 6, 2021, Tennessee was visiting Kentucky. It was a tight game into the fourth quarter. Tennessee led 38-35 with 13:40 remaining. Kentucky had the ball, and it was second down and twenty-one yards to go. I was standing behind the center, waiting for the teams to complete their substitution process. When my referee gave me the signal that the substitution was complete, I moved to take my normal position behind the quarterback.

What I didn't know was that Kentucky wide receiver Chauncey Magwood was running in motion across the formation. I took one step backward and WHAM! He smoked me, hitting me square in the back. I never saw it coming.

Here's the thing: we officials keep getting older. But these big, strong, fast football players are always between the ages of eighteen and twenty-two. They're also wearing shoulder pads and a helmet, while the only thing I have protecting me is my thick skull.

Officiating carries physical risks all over the field, but officials who work the umpire position—which is on the defensive side of the ball behind the linebackers—are the most vulnerable. Most running plays come right at them, and receivers will often use them to try and scrape off defenders on a passing route.

On September 9, 2023, I was fortunate enough to work the game between Alabama and Texas in Tuscaloosa. It was an awesome night—one of the biggest games of the year, at night, under the lights, broadcasted on national television. The place was loaded with politicians, athletes from other sports, and (of course) Matthew McConaughey.

In the middle of the third quarter, it was fourth down, and Alabama was going to punt from their own forty-one-yard line. On punts and kickoffs, players can hit full speed in about three strides and maintain that speed while they are engaged with an opponent who is blocking them the entire way down the field. On this particular play, my umpire had four players coming straight at him from two different angles.

He was able to maneuver around the first pair of players, but that put him directly in the path of the other two: Texas defender Gavin Holmes and Alabama wide receiver Kendrick Law, who was sprinting down the field to cover the punt. My umpire got violently knocked to the ground and received a cut to his face after getting hit by Law's helmet. He was okay, but he had to sit out for a few plays to get the proper medical care and to collect himself.

So, guess what I got to do?

As my umpire recovered on the sideline, I moved to umpire to take his place, trying my best to fill in for him for several plays. In my normal position of center judge, I stand behind the quarterback and observe all the action as it moves *away* from me. Now, it was all coming straight at me. I was more than a little anxious.

Texas had the ball at their own six-yard line. Normally, the umpire stands about eight to ten yards beyond the ball, near the linebackers. For self-preservation purposes, I lined up more like fifteen yards away. After the game, several of my officiating friends were teasing me that I was closer to the back judge, who stands twenty-five yards downfield.

I worked six terrifying plays that night as an umpire. It seemed like much more, and I have to say, my career as an umpire is done. I can't fully express my relief when the medical staff cleared my colleague to return to his duties.

The physical strain of officiating isn't limited to injuries you may incur during a football game. Over time, the challenges on the body take their toll. Again, the players stay young, but we get older. In 2007, shortly after he retired from the NFL, Michael Strahan said that he believed he was still at the top of his game and could still dominate, but getting out of bed the morning after a game was sometimes physically impossible.

Now, by no means am I comparing myself to an NFL Hall of Famer. But there have been plenty of times when, the morning after a game, I look at a flight of stairs and have to really think about how I'm going to get up or down them.

As you get older, sometimes stuff just happens. In November 2022, my wife and I were parking at the Phoenix airport to catch a flight to my last game of the season, LSU at Texas A&M. As I got out of my pickup truck, I told my wife I was having an odd feeling in my back. By the time we arrived at the hotel and had dinner, I was having trouble getting up from a seated position.

When I woke up on Saturday morning, I was no better. Everything was difficult—getting out of bed, showering, walking. I didn't even want to try sitting down because I knew there was no way I could get back up.

I was able to get most of my uniform on before the game, everything except for my shoes and socks. There was just no way. I couldn't position my body to reach my feet without excruciating pain. If you ever want a humbling experience, get to a point in your life where you are unable to dress yourself. I didn't tell my wife this at the time, but it brought me to tears. I was sitting on the floor trying to put on my shoes, crying because of the pain and because I couldn't complete a simple personal care task on my own.

I had no idea how I was going to work the game.

We rode over to the stadium, and I told my crewmates that it was very possible that I was not going to be able to work. But my umpire was a former NFL player, and he knew exactly what to do. He took me to one of the team doctors, and they injected me with Toradol, a pain-killing anti-inflammatory.

I got the shot about two hours before kickoff, and I was still limping around until game time. But once that ball was kicked, the Toradol—along with some adrenaline, probably—took effect, and all the pain left my body. With the physical pounding we had all taken over the course of the season, that was the best I'd felt in months. We worked a solid game with no issues.

Then I woke up the next morning.

The Toradol had worn off. The adrenaline was gone. I had honestly probably hurt my back even worse during the game, but the Toradol had been masking it. If it weren't for my wife and a couple of our friends who came to help us (thanks, Chris and Lori Conway), I think I might still be in that hotel bed in College Station. My wife dressed me and packed up all our stuff, and our friends drove our rental car back for us. Of course, on the drive back to the airport, Murphy's Law struck, and we got a flat tire. I was no help. At the airport, my wife found a wheelchair and had to push me through the airport and get me on and off airplanes. And when we finally got home to Phoenix, my doctor informed me that I had two herniated lumbar discs.

Two weeks later, I was awarded a bowl game. It was an incredible honor, and it was probably the very last thing I needed. It was the 2022 Fiesta Bowl, scheduled for December 31 between Michigan and Texas Christian University. Not only was it a bowl game, it was the semifinals of the College Football Playoff, and the winner would advance to play in the National Championship. My back was *not* better at this point. But no matter how bad I hurt, only a team of horses could have pulled me away from that one.

For the entire month of December, I rested and rehabbed as best I could. On the day of the game, I wasn't feeling much better, so I thought I'd give Toradol another try after it had helped so much last time. It did nothing for me at all. This was one of the biggest games in my career, and all I could do was wonder how I was going to get through it.

I worked the first half of the game in extreme pain. Enough adrenaline kicked in that I was able to function and work effectively, but I was miserable. Every play, I'd put the ball on the ground, and then I wanted to scream out in pain as I backpedaled to my center judge position. I began to realize that the game deserved better than what I could give it. I also realized that there was someone standing on the sideline who was fully capable of doing better.

Our alternate official for the game was Scott Walker, who is now an official in the NFL. During his time in the SEC, though, he had acted as referee and center judge—my position. And he was exceptional at it.

At halftime, I told Scott that I couldn't continue and the rest of the game was his. It broke my heart to give up on one of the biggest games of my career because I couldn't perform physically, but I knew I owed it to the players, the coaches, and the fans to make sure the game was officiated properly. It's a good thing I made the choice I did. The second half was a track meet, with the teams scoring a combined sixty-nine points. Scott and I switched at the right time, it was seamless, and the game was better for it.

Leaving that game, I couldn't walk. Luckily for me, though, the Fiesta Bowl was in Glendale, Arizona, which was only about twenty minutes from our home in Phoenix. I went home, and I could barely function physically. That's when I understood that if I don't eventually decide when I'm done with football, my body will decide for me.

I spent the next six months getting epidural steroid injections from a neurologist and spine specialist, plus physical therapy, rehab, and plenty of stretching. I'm not getting any younger, but at least for now, I'm not ready to quit.

What's the best game you've ever worked?

This is one of the more common questions I get, and there are layers to the answer.

I've been lucky to work in some great conferences—the Big Ten, the SEC, the MAC, and the Sun Belt. I've been a part of some amazing games, including bowl games and championship games. I've had the privilege of seeing a lot of memorable moments in a lot of amazing places with Heisman Trophy winners and finalists.

Still, with all of that, this is my honest answer: the best game is any game that I get to work with my crew where we give it everything we have for three and a half hours and absolutely nail it. There's no other place I'd rather be on a Saturday afternoon than in the middle of the field, surrounded by one hundred thousand people who all believe their team deserves to be the national champion (even if that team has a losing record). And running off the field when the clock hits zero and knowing I left it all out there is amazing. I get to experience it eleven times each fall—maybe twelve or thirteen if they need me for an additional regular-season game or if I'm lucky enough to get postseason assignments. There's nothing like it.

That being said, some games stand out. Getting assigned to a bowl game or a conference championship game is like a celebration, an affirmation of the hard work you put in all season. It doesn't matter if you're working a New Year's Six bowl game or the lowest bowl game on the schedule, it's a special feeling. If you get to work it alongside one of your crewmates with whom you climbed the eleven-game mountain of the regular season, it's even better. I had this privilege in 2012 when I worked the MAC Championship Game in Detroit alongside three of my regular-season crewmates (plus two other officials who were good friends of mine). That game was an amazing, memorable experience, not because of what happened in the game or which teams were involved, but because I got to work it with people who meant so much to me.

One of my most memorable games (and definitely one of the most meaningful) happened at the end of the 2023 season. It was a solid season for our crew overall, and as we neared the end, some good rumors were going around about what postseason assignments some of us might get. Generally, you can't believe these rumors because no one truly knows who's going where. Too many factors are involved. Still, it was hard not to get my hopes up.

On Saturday, November 18, I worked my last regular-season game, and when I got home, I tossed my football bag on the ground next to our washing machine and forgot about it. Football consumes so much time during the season that when you finally get to the end of a season, it's nice to just disconnect from it for a little while.

Then, on November 26, the texts started. "Congrats!" "Way to go!" "Super happy for you!"

Was it possible? I was honestly scared to even look.

But it was true.

I had been awarded the 2023 SEC Championship Game, which would be between Georgia and Alabama. Better yet, I was going to work it with two of my crewmates from the regular season, and the rest of our crew was going to be at the game in Atlanta to support us.

It ended up being an incredible game, living up to the hype of the matchup. Alabama won 27-24, becoming SEC champions in the process and moving on to the College Football Playoff. But what stood out to me most about that game was the same as what stands out to me about every game I officiate. It was an honor to be trusted to officiate such an important matchup. What I remember most was sharing it with my officiating brothers who had been on the journey with me—the ones who had climbed the mountain alongside me, who had gone through the grind of driving all over the Southeast to work practices and scrimmages in the August heat and hung tough over the course of a long season. Together, we had pushed through booing fans, screaming coaches, and a dozen television cameras staring us in the face multiple times a game.

Much more than the game itself, that's what I remember. I remember the people I got to share it with.

So why do you do it?

It's simple: we do it because we love it. We are fueled by the challenge of it. It's a two-hundred-play puzzle. Within those two hundred plays, there are twenty-two one-on-one matchups that we need to assess. Within each of those individual matchups, we are weighing who has the advantage or disadvantage and whether they achieved it fairly and within what the rules allow. We do it knowing that at the end of the game, there will be at least one play that we will beat ourselves up over, wishing we would've worked better. That motivates us to prepare even harder for the next week.

We get to prepare for an entire week to go to another fantastic college football stadium every weekend in the fall, to be on the field for three and a half hours, for sixty minutes of game time with our officiating team. We are willing to take on an extreme amount of accountability that most others won't. It's a collaborative bond that you rarely find in the money-focused corporate world. College football officiating is all about managing a game as fairly and equitably as possible for the teams, coaching staffs, schools, and millions of fans watching us in real time.

Why do I do it? Better question: How could I not?

PART 2

LESSONS FROM THE FIELD

NOW THAT I'VE shared my story with you, I'd like to spend the rest of this book sharing some of the lessons I've learned and some of the attributes that have been most important to my success as an official. I hope they'll give you a bit of insight into what it takes to officiate football at the highest level, and I encourage you to read with an open mind about how you might apply some of these same lessons to your own life.

CHAPTER 7

RELATIONSHIPS

AS I WAS putting this book together, I strongly considered making this the very first chapter of my book. That's how important relationships have been to me in my career and how important I believe they are across all situations in life. So, when I decided to focus the second half of my book on the most important elements of my success as an official, I knew there was no other place to start.

I'll put it simply: relationships are the most critical aspect of anything we achieve in life. They make us who we are.

When I retire from officiating, the number-one thing I'm going to miss won't be the game, the bright lights, or the historic stadiums. It definitely won't be calling holding fouls or talking to angry coaches on the sideline. The thing I'll miss most is being with my friends, my officiating brothers who are by my side for fourteen Saturdays out of the year (and then some).

When I first got into officiating high school football, before I had even finished college, the men I worked alongside were the first group of true adult friends I'd ever had in my life. Other than my grandfather, they were the only positive male influences I'd had in my life to that point. Our personal lives weren't separate from our football lives—they were intertwined. These men were alongside me, and they kept me on the right path.

Now, I'm grateful to no longer be directionless like I was in my younger days, but the relationships with my crew are exactly the same quality they were back then. We're not just coworkers or crewmates. We're genuinely friends, invested in each other's lives. We care about each other. I got into football because I loved the game, but these relationships keep my heart in it even more than the excitement of stepping onto the field every Saturday during the season.

In college football, our crew consists of eight on-field officials and two replay officials, and for most of the year, that group stays the same. We're together for the entire year—for football season, of course, but also during the offseason. I usually talk or text with most members of my crew several times throughout the week even during the offseason. We vacation together, go to each other's weddings, go to sporting events together, and support each other in business and charity functions.

One of my favorite annual traditions is getting together with a group in February for the sole purpose of making fun of each other. Over the course of the season, we collect game film of plays where someone does something silly during a game. Usually, it's stuff that no one else would even notice, like lining up in the wrong spot, but sometimes we catch each other tripping over our own feet, getting knocked over by a player who is running full speed, or getting hit in the face by a pass. Moments like that allow us to laugh together and bond like a family. They remind me how good I have it.

The people whom I've met through my officiating journey are some of the best people I've ever known. They've helped me in my career. I wouldn't be where I am without them, and I wouldn't be half the official I am without their help and guidance. They've set an example for me to follow and learn from. They've supported me along the way when I've needed it, encouraged me, given me great advice, and helped me immensely in growing my career.

This chapter is for them. I can't talk about every single person who's impacted my officiating journey because that would fill an entire book. But I'm going to talk about a few people who have impacted me, what I learned from them, and how I hope to be a little more like them in my officiating work.

As you read, have your own story in the back of your mind. Who in your own life has contributed to your personal success and development? How has that impacted you? How could you play that role for someone else?

Marc Curles

Sometimes, you're lucky enough to work with certain people who make you realize, even in the moment, that you're lucky to be there with them. Marc Curles is one of those people for me.

From 2017 through 2021, Marc was the referee on my crew. He set the tone for our crew with his smooth, calm demeanor, which made us feel like there was never anything he (or we as a crew) couldn't handle. With Marc, it didn't matter whether he had made the greatest call of all time or if he was second-guessing himself, his attitude always stayed the same. He was steady, confident, and a great example for our crew of how to officiate.

Off the field, Marc is the kind of guy you'd want your son, brother, or best friend to be. He is kind, is generous with his time, and never has a bad word to say about anyone. I've personally experienced this from Marc more than once. He's helped encourage me in my faith, setting an example of what it looks like to put the Lord first and lean on Him for guidance. And he's been there to support me when I've struggled. There was a time not long ago when it felt like I was headed in the wrong direction in many areas of my personal life, and Marc was the first person I called. He helped me get back on the right path.

Simply put, I try to be more like Marc. I'm not great at it, but I am trying. I don't have his patience or his ability to stay calm in every situation, but watching him inspires me to be better.

I think about games when he was my referee and he would talk to a head coach during a TV timeout. The coach would ask Marc about a ruling, and Marc would very clearly articulate the rule and how we determined the outcome. The coach would then absolutely erupt with anger because the ruling wasn't going his way. I'll talk about this more later in this book, but staying calm in those situations is essential as an official, and Marc was the expert in finding ways of removing himself from those heated moments without having any reaction at all. I am not nearly as skilled as he is with this.

I remember one specific game between Kentucky and Mississippi State when an extremely unhappy coach called Marc over to the sideline. The memory of Marc standing calmly on the sideline, listening to the coach yell at him while staying completely calm, giving no reaction at all, is permanently etched in my brain. The instinct for most people would be to turn to the coach and try to defend their position, digging themselves a deeper hole and making the situation unnecessarily confrontational. After listening to the coach's heated comments, Marc simply looked at the coach and said, "Coach, this conversation is no longer productive." Then he calmly walked away and resumed his on-field duties. I wish I had that skill.

During the five years we worked together, Marc was like my partner on the field. Most officials on the field have a corresponding partner they communicate with most often, and with the close proximity of our positions—center judge and referee—it was natural for us to check in with each other on plays to make sure we were observing the same thing. My work supported his, and he depended on me. I did my job so he could do his, especially when he was announcing fouls or results of replay reviews. If I failed, I was failing him, and he trusted me with that. That trust and the accountability that came with it made me work harder and become a better official.

Marc Curles is one of the best officials I've ever worked with, and working with him in the SEC has made me a better official and a better person.

Jeff Servinski

Some people impact you over time. Others impact you in a moment that sticks with you forever. That's Jeff Servinski for me.

When I was hired as a referee in the GLIAC in 2008, it was my first time being assigned that position full-time on a college football officiating crew. The referee isn't just the one who gets to announce fouls during the game—they are the leader of the crew, the person who communicates most frequently with the supervisor, and the one the crew members come to with questions or issues. I felt comfortable enough working the position, but it was new to me, and I was very open to advice.

That's where Jeff came in. When I joined the GLIAC, he was also working as a referee, and now he's in the Big Ten, working the same position. He gave me some advice that has served me well ever since in both football and business. "After every game," he said, "call the supervisor. Let him know how the game went, and *always* have something positive to say about the crew's performance."

This became my new rule of thumb for any team I lead, inside or outside of football: always tell the person in charge what's going on, and *always* have an example ready to share of how the members of the team are doing excellent work to push things forward. Before I started my own business, I would send my manager an "every Friday email," which I'd use to recap the week, letting him know what I'd been up to and highlighting the good work of the salespeople and support staff whom I worked with.

Want to improve morale and culture at the office? Brag about your coworkers.

I've seen such huge results from this one simple piece of advice. We live in a negative feedback society, which can be completely draining for both energy and morale. It feels like there's always somebody in management whose feedback comes from a negative perspective. Jeff taught me to be better than that.

Jeff's advice changed my entire paradigm around what leadership looks like. He taught me to always lead in a positive manner. Football officiating is hard. You can choose to pick on the negatives, or you can choose to look at the positive things and say, "Wow, if we do more of this positive stuff, more great things happen."

This doesn't mean that we ignore things that need to be fixed. But it made sense easily in my mind. If I keep talking to you about the great things you're doing, you're going to keep doing those great things. If I keep picking on the negative stuff, you're going to think I'm a jerk and likely won't perform at your best level.

That one lesson about positive leadership from Jeff stuck with me. We never worked on the same crew, but I'll never forget the way he impacted my life.

Jay Brown

On April 26, 2021, the SEC announced that it was bringing in four new officials to fill vacancies left by officials who had retired. And for a lot of us, me included, there was one name we all hoped to see announced as one of those new officials: Jay Brown.

Jay had been officiating football since 1984, and he'd spent the previous eleven years in the Sun Belt Conference. Moving up from the Sun Belt to the SEC was often a natural progression for officials, and it doesn't matter who you are or where you work, eleven years is a long time to go without that next step.

Jay had done all the right things. He always worked hard, and he knew the rules better than most. He created practice exams, and—the most classic "Jay Brown" thing of all—he ran a study group where he welcomed any and all officials to come and work on their knowledge of the rules, regardless of what level they officiated or how many years of experience they had. Jay's study group was so good that those who attended regularly were typically among the best scorers on rules tests in their respective conferences.

Despite all of that, though, Jay had been passed over time and time again when new officials were being hired in the SEC. And when the SEC made their announcement on April 26, 2021, the day came and went with no phone call.

Here's the reality: most football officials don't get to be on staff of a conference at the level of the SEC, Big Ten, Big 12, or ACC. There are only so many spots, and there are no guarantees. Even for those who do make it, they're staring down at least a ten-year journey from working fifth-grade games in the rain for seven dollars, then high school, then smaller college games, then smaller Division I conferences before they'd even have a chance to be considered for a major conference. Few make it that far. I almost quit myself before making it to the Big Ten.

But Jay had stuck it out. He'd shown hard work and dedication. He'd gone out of his way to help other people advance, even though he wasn't advancing himself. He did everything right. And now, he was about to be passed over for the twelfth year in a row.

On promotion day on April 26, Jay's phone didn't ring. Then, on April 27, it did.

It was the SEC supervisor of officials. Jay's wait was over. After a total of thirty-seven years as an official, it was finally his time. He had advanced to the SEC, the top of the mountain for him (as it is for most of us).

Every year that Jay had been passed over, he became an example of somebody who was determined to continue giving their best effort even in the face of rejection. He set an incredible example for me of what kind of person I want to be—not just in football, but in life. He continued to control the things he could control, and eventually, he got what we all knew he had deserved for so long.

I owe a lot in my career to Jay. His selfless work in putting together his study group helped me become proficient with my rules. In fact, I consistently score at the top, and I've gotten a perfect score on my last four SEC rules exams (thanks, Jay!). Even now that he's in the SEC, he continues his study group for people of all levels. He's created an environment where everyone can learn, from SEC veterans to high school officials trying to break into college. It's just who he is, and not only have I learned a lot about officiating football from his tests, but I've also learned a lot about being a good person from his example.

Every season that I'm fortunate enough to earn a bowl game, I call Jay and thank him the day before I go out and take the field. I know I wouldn't be there without him.

Greg Blum

Greg was my referee in the MAC. He is a "guy's guy," meaning he knows how to be a leader in a room full of testosterone. He is quick with the wisecracks and can be the target of them as well. Because of him, our crew was never short on laughter. We once had a game at the University of Massachusetts, and all of us went a day early to tour Boston. That day ranks on my "Mount Rushmore" of days, one of the top four days in my life when it comes to laughter and memorable experiences. One of my favorite fun facts about Greg is that he would invite other officials over to his house for rules discussions, and he would go out into the yard and use bags of flour to draw yard lines in the grass to create a tiny football field so they could practice.

In the summer of 2009, I received a bulky envelope in the mail from some unknown city in either Nebraska or Iowa. When I opened it, I found the book *LEAD...for God's Sake* by Todd G. Gongwer. It's the first book that truly reached me on a deeper level. I am not going to spoil the ending, but I will share this with you: Gongwer has a great way of illustrating how to worry only about the things you have full control over. Everything else will take care of itself. I encourage you to read it.

The crew eventually deduced that Greg had sent this book to all of us. It had such an impact on me that I borrowed his trick, and I anonymously sent my crew the book *Power of a Positive Team* by Jon Gordon. Greg's action was the catalyst for me to read more books like this, become certified to teach leadership and teamwork, and create my own leadership consulting firm.

Bill LeMonnier

The last person I want to highlight in this chapter is a living legend in the officiating world: Bill LeMonnier.

Bill was a longtime referee in the Big Ten, and I was on his crew for my very first game as a full-time Division I official (the Penn State game I mentioned earlier where I felt the ground shake beneath my feet). On the Wednesday before the game, my phone rang at nine o'clock at night. I couldn't imagine who would be calling me so late in the evening, but I looked at my phone and saw it was an out-of-town number with a Chicago area code.

Believing it was a telemarketer, I answered the phone in my grumpiest, most aggressive voice. "Hello, and who is this?!"

The voice on the other end of the phone was so sincere and kind that it completely caught me off guard. "Hello, Chris!" the man said. "This is Bill LeMonnier."

I had just given my grumpy greeting to a football officiating legend in the Big Ten, and possibly the entire country. I slapped my forehead with my other hand and started apologizing as quickly as I could.

Bill knew that this game was my first Big Ten assignment. He also knew that I was about as nervous as a long-tailed cat in a room full of rocking chairs. So, he wanted to talk to me about logistics and what would be expected of me in the game (I was supposed to work as the alternate official). He also gave me a chance to ask any questions I had. He didn't need to call me. He definitely didn't need to stay on the phone with me after my rude greeting. He could have just let me figure it out on my own. But he didn't. He took the time to help a rookie D-I official feel comfortable in his first game of the year.

That's the only time I've ever worked on a crew with Bill in my career. Now I'm in the SEC, and he's working on TV as a football rules analyst for a major network. Once a year or so, he'll be assigned to work one of my games, and he always stops by the locker room to say hi to everyone.

Bill still mentors young officials, just like he reached out to offer mentorship to me on that day. Every time I see him, I'm reminded of my humble beginnings in officiating. I remember what it was like to be new and inexperienced and how much it meant to me that a veteran like Bill would take time out of his day to reach out to me. It's a reminder of how much I owe to people like Bill for helping me get to where I am now, and I want to provide that same kind of support for other up-and-coming officials whenever I can.

I have no doubt that without the people who have helped me along my officiating journey, I'd be out of football. I would have retired after my sixth year of D-III football, if I'd even made it that far. The people who have helped me along the way are the reason I've made it as far as I have. And the strong relationships I've formed with my colleagues are the reasons I've been able to continue growing and working at a high level year after year.

It's not just football, though. I wouldn't be anywhere near the person I am if I hadn't met the people I have on my officiating journey. You can't officiate football and be shady or deceitful, so I am surrounded by people who are honest, fair, and full of integrity. In the most difficult circumstances, they have the ability to pause and consciously decide to do the right thing. That wasn't always natural for me. But now, thanks to them, I can do it, too.

The people I've gotten to know through football have helped me grow into a leader. From my time in the Navy, I'd known I had an aptitude for leadership, but I'd never really taken the time to invest and grow my leadership abilities. On the football field, I got to learn alongside these men every single snap, demonstrating courage and leadership as we assessed plays, communicated with each other, interacted with players, and made decisions 197 times every Saturday of the season.

In football, in work, and in life, I have no doubt relationships are everything.

On your journey of life and pathway to success, who has impacted you most? Who has helped you get to where you are today? What have you learned from them? Whom could you reach out to and thank for the impact they've had on your life? What could you do to reach out and have that same kind of impact on others?

CHAPTER 8

PREPARATION

WHEN YOU OFFICIATE in the SEC, you spend most of your Saturdays during football season knowing one hundred thousand fans are watching in the stadium and millions more are watching on TV who are prepared to hold you personally responsible if they feel their team is even the least bit slighted. TV broadcasters are ready to point out every mistake you make to the entire world, and football coaches roaming the sideline are ready to share their thoughts with you in a manner that some may describe as "not very nice." It would be enough to make most normal people pretty nervous.

This is why, to officiate football at the highest level, you have to put in an immense amount of preparation.

I don't get nervous anymore when I officiate even the biggest college football games. That's not a boast—it's just a fact, and for a very good reason. Do I get anxious? Excited? Do I want to do a great job? Yes, to all of those things. I'm not nervous for Saturday, though, because of all the hard work I do Monday through Friday of game week, not to mention everything we do in the six months leading up to the start of football season. What spectators see during the sixty minutes of game action on a Saturday is simply the end product of over a thousand hours of preparation that literally started months before.

In this chapter, I'm going to provide a closer look at that preparation. People will sometimes ask me what a day in the life of an official is like, but I'm going to provide a look at a year in the life of an official. I'll walk through what our offseason looks like, and then what each day of the week looks like when we get to football season.

I believe preparation is the key to success in officiating, and I believe its impact extends to so many other areas of life. Without the level of preparation I put in as an official, I wouldn't last a day in the SEC, and I certainly wouldn't be invited to officiate a bowl game or conference championship game.

As a result of my preparation work, I'm able to enter into high-stress environments and bring my A game.

The Offseason

After the last bowl games are finished in January, I put my football stuff away and try not to think about it for a month. That's my offseason. After that, it's time to start getting prepared for the next season (which officially starts in August).

In late January/early February, we have one-on-one evaluation calls with our supervisor, who is in charge of officiating for all of the SEC. In our case, that supervisor is John McDaid. John is a Harvard graduate, which I say to demonstrate something that's clear to all of us who work under him: no matter what, John is always the smartest one in the room. It's more than a little intimidating to have a performance assessment with someone you know right out of the gate is smarter than you and sees things at a higher and usually more complex level than you see them.

Going into this review, I always try to do my prep work. I look at my metrics from the previous season, which include my score from the National NCAA and SEC rules exams I took the previous July, my weekly quiz scores, and my grade reports containing evaluations of each individual play from each game I worked.

In the review itself, John walks through the numbers with me. How many correct calls did I make? How many incorrect calls? How many non-quality calls did I make, meaning calls that might be technically correct but shouldn't have been called because they had no impact on the play? Are my mechanics correct, meaning did I move to the correct place as the play developed to be able to see and assess it properly?

Then, John and I have an honest conversation about my numbers. How did I do compared to the previous season? How did my performance improve or decline as the season went along? What areas of improvement could I focus on for the upcoming season?

For example, in my most recent conversation with John (after the 2023 season), we identified together that I started the season strong and then went on a streak of three games where I missed a call or two each game. It wasn't because I wasn't seeing the action. I was evaluating them as not being big enough or having enough of an effect on the play. I got back on track and finished the rest of the season strong, and I ended up with only three or four missed calls for the season. Of the 1,873 plays I officiated that season, that's a 99.997864 percent rate of accuracy. Not terrible, right? But it eats me alive. Even if the missed calls don't end up impacting the result of the game (and for me, they never have), the fact I missed them drives me crazy.

So, in my meeting with John, his coaching with me for the 2024 season was simple: continue to lower my bar for the threshold of a foul. Meaning don't relax. I had been missing fouls because, in my mind, they weren't "big" enough. But the reality was, as I reviewed the film, they had been big enough.

After meeting with John, I begin implementing his advice and reviewing game film from the previous season. I "re-officiate" the games and reinforce the new guidance I received from John. So, for 2024, I went into the season knowing I had to have a lower tolerance for offensive holding, illegal hits on the quarterback, and blocking below the waist. When mid-season hits, I have to resist any urge to relax my standard. I won't make it my goal to call more fouls, but I am determined to stay consistent and call the fouls that are there and have an impact on the play.

In March, the upcoming season begins in earnest. We start by having spring football meetings, which are conducted over the course of several nights via Zoom. These are huge meetings, with over two hundred people in some cases, attending from two or three conferences and maybe even more, depending on the part of the country the attendees are in.

We spend time as a group reviewing what went well in the previous season, what improvements we should focus on in the upcoming season, and any proposed rule changes that are set to be voted on later in April. These rule changes can happen in a variety of ways as the game evolves:

- Some rule changes are motivated by player safety, like the creation of the blindside block, targeting, and expanding horse-collar tackles as fouls.
- Some changes are motivated by the way the game is played from a strategic standpoint. For example, some teams would play offense with no huddles or substitutions, get the defense

on their heels, and then quickly substitute a fast wide receiver for a big tight end to gain a matchup advantage before the defense had the chance to respond. Now, as a result, if the offense makes a substitution, the defense must be given time to make a substitution as well.

- Some changes are simply the result of the progression and evolution of the game. For example, a 2024 rule change allowed a one-way radio in a player's helmet for the coach to communicate with him while he is on the field.
- Other rule changes are made to try to improve the game as a whole. For example, in the 2024 season, a new "two-minute timeout" was introduced. It is similar to the NFL's two-minute warning. College football has always existed without this timeout, but it was added so that football fans will have a more consistent experience across the different football games they watch, which could improve their experience watching college games.

Based on everything we learn in those initial preseason meetings, we get very quickly into film study. For certain segments, we watch and discuss plays as an entire group. Then we break out into smaller groups for more discussion based on the positions we work on the field. Those positions (along with some of their primary responsibilities) are:

- Referee: wears the white hat and makes the announcements.
- Center judge (my position): lines up behind the offense with the referee and controls the pace of team substitutions, which allows both teams to match up fairly.
- Head line judge and line judge: line up on either sideline on the line of scrimmage and ensure the offense lines up and starts each play correctly.

- Umpire: lines up in the middle of the field behind the defense (and gets knocked down most often!).
- Side judge, field judge, and back judge: line up deep behind the defense, primarily watching for fouls that occur on pass and punt plays.

In each of these groups, we dive even deeper, talking about our specific responsibilities on different plays and how we should respond in different situations that might come up. It's one of the best chances in the entire year to dig into how best to succeed in your position with others who do the same thing. We review rules and scenarios to prepare for the upcoming season and the weekly series of spring quizzes we'll receive starting shortly after these meetings begin.

Around this same time, schools start their spring practices. They all want officials to come to these practices and help both players and coaches learn the new rules that will be implemented in the coming season and to ask questions and gain awareness of any team playing issues that need to be shored up.

These practices are great opportunities for us as officials to sharpen our skills. Many of us work as many spring practices as we can. It's all about getting snaps, repetition, and extra training for your eyes to all the visual cues you need to be looking for when you're watching the action at game speed. All of this culminates in April when many schools have some type of spring game, which can be a big event at some schools (especially in the SEC).

Generally speaking, the months of May and June are known as dead months in college football. Spring practices are over, and fall practices don't start until the beginning of August.

But for officials, it's a much different story. April through July are the months when we have to start ramping up our physical fitness training if we're going to be ready for the season. We're about to spend every Saturday of the fall running around the field after players who are decades younger than we are, so it's time to get serious about shedding the weight we put on over the winter months and get ready to deal with the physical demands that officiating puts on our bodies.

As a center judge, I run about eight miles each game—about half of it backward. In games between teams that play fast and run more plays over the course of a game, that number can creep closer to ten miles. No one will ever catch me competing in a marathon, but in April through July, I have to log the miles to make sure I can last through four full quarters. I put in time in the gym, go out on summer runs to acclimate to the heat, and pay close attention to my diet to make sure what I'm putting into my body will serve me during the upcoming season.

I distinctly remember a game early in my SEC career at Mississippi State. It was hot (as most SEC games are), and by the time we got to the fourth quarter, I was completely out of gas. I was struggling to keep up physically. My lack of conditioning negatively impacted our crew as well as me, and by the end of the game, I only had one thought in my head: never again. Never again would I voluntarily put myself in a position where I physically could not keep up. If I was injured, fine. But I decided that would be the last time I would fail physically because I was out of shape.

So, I go outside and run. I eat the best I can. I go to the gym. And when it gets tough, I think about that day in Starkville, Mississippi, and I'll do one more rep. One more exercise. One more set. Even if it's just a few more sit-ups, I am driven to improve every single time and to prepare my body just as hard as I prepare my mind for the upcoming season.

May, June, and July are also very heavy study and practice-test-taking months. After the proposed rule changes are finalized and voted on in April, weekly quizzes come out from the first week of May through the middle of July to help us get familiar with the new rules. We also take a one-hundred-question rules test published every year during this time by College Football Officiating LLC, the national governing body of college football officials. If you want to be considered for a postseason assignment, you must achieve a minimum passing score on this exam, and let's just say it's in an official's best interest to go ahead and score 100 percent.

Between all the studying and quizzes during the early summer months, we're also having frequent calls with peers and conference calls with our entire officiating crew to make sure we're all on the same page on rule changes and any other points of emphasis for the upcoming season. When I tell you we pore over thousands of football play scenarios from the beginning of May through the end of July, I'm probably understating it. We're constantly in the rule book, constantly watching film, and constantly reaching out to each other to make sure we all understand things in the same way.

During the last week of July, officials from three conferences—the Sun Belt, Southern, and SEC—all come together in Birmingham. Other conferences gather together in their geographic areas as well in a similar fashion.

At this meeting, we take the conference rules exam put together by our supervisor. The expectations are high. There's peer pressure from every direction because every single person in the room wants to score 100 percent. If that's not someone's target, then they don't belong in that room. Average isn't good enough. An A-minus will be enough to all but guarantee the official won't be assigned a bowl game this season.

After the exam, we spend two days studying game film. Examining game film is the heart and soul of how we improve as officials, and while we've been doing it together for the past few months at this point, it's different when we're in the same room together. We can eyeball each other. The mental grinding happening around the room is palpable. Nobody wants to be the one to get a question wrong, to crack under the pressure while their position specialist and supervisor are firing questions at them.

But the point of these meetings isn't just to be right or wrong. It's deeper than that. It's about gaining a better understanding of how to officiate the different plays we see, but more importantly, it's about identifying *why*. It's about identifying hidden complexities in a play that appears basic at its beginning and preparing to respond to new innovations that coaching staffs are constantly putting in place as the game evolves. We challenge each other to be better in these meetings, and we all come out better.

As soon as we leave Birmingham on that last Saturday in July, football season rockets into action. Schools begin football practices the following week, and throughout most of August, we work at least two days per week on average at schools, continuing to get in as many reps as possible. Practically every school wants us to come to practice, watch their players, and speak to their staffs about rule changes for the upcoming season. Some are working on plays that they know are right on the edge of what the rules allow, and they want our input.

For me, by the time the season starts, I like to believe I've already seen enough practice and scrimmage time to fill four or five full games. This helps me start the season feeling like I'm already in mid-season form. Any rust I might have felt a few months ago is gone now. We begin working on the field in uniform in early August—it just so happens that our first game doesn't come until September.

Game Week

Typically, the first Saturday in September—or, as we call it, week one—brings our first game. Once we reach this point, our typical game week gets into a standard cadence. Here's what that looks like.

Sunday is game film review day. We spend this day reviewing in extreme detail every single play from the previous week's game. I watch each play about six times, observing something different each time:

1   First, I simply watch the play. What happened? Does anything appear suspect right off the bat?

2   I watch my movement. Did I move in the right direction based on what happened in the play? Am I looking at the right areas?

3   I look at players for whom I have primary responsibility. Did I officiate them properly, or did they do something that I didn't catch in live action?

4   I observe the action that takes place away from the player who has the football. Did I miss a late hit or some type of unsportsmanlike conduct?

5   I track administrative tasks. Did we start and stop the clock correctly? If there were penalties, did we mark them off properly and efficiently?

6   Finally, I watch how the rest of the crew performs. We all hold each other accountable to do our best work on each play, so I watch the play to see if there's feedback I can provide a member of my team. It is the responsibility of each of us to hold the others accountable.

I watch every play at game speed and in slow motion. We have software that provides us with multiple camera angles we can view. What we see from our position on the field can look much different from another angle.

On Monday morning, we spend time exchanging texts and phone calls with the other members of our crew, sharing our opinions of the previous game and getting on the same page on what we did well and what we need to improve. We also receive our weekly rules test, which we need to complete and bring with us to that week's game site.

Let me pause and address a question you may be asking at this point: Why so many tests?

People are always surprised about how much work goes into being an official at the highest level of college football. Football rules are complex, multifaceted, and multilayered. It is absolutely unacceptable for an official not to know the rule, how to identify it, and how to properly enforce it. There's no room for "we'll do it better next time." No one wants to hear about an officiating error deciding the game. So, the game demands that we be elite rules experts. If there's a question, we have to know the answer. And telling a coach, "I'm not sure, let me get back to the office and send you a follow-up email," is not on the list of acceptable answers.

And the only way to know the answer every single time is through practice, preparation, and rehearsal—going through it a hundred times before we ever step on a football field on Saturday. There are too many things going on to trust that we'll remember everything from week to week. We need to be constantly testing ourselves to keep the knowledge we need right at the front of our minds where we need it. Our testing starts in March, and it doesn't stop until the second weekend of December. It doesn't let up, nor should it.

Here's one of my favorite Nick Saban quotes: "It's not practicing until you get it right. It's practicing it so much you can't get it wrong." That perfectly describes why we approach our rules tests with such extreme discipline. We are tested constantly to ensure that every time we see a situation on the field, we get it right.

Midweek, our grades arrive. Yes, that's right—grades. This is one of the most important elements of my job as an official, but very few people know about it. Each official is evaluated and graded on every single play of the game. Our performance is graded on multiple areas and by multiple people:

- First, as individual officials, we self-evaluate our own plays—the fouls we called and any other play of note where something happened that we needed to address. You may be wondering if we give ourselves a perfect score each time. We certainly don't. We put too much work into it to not be honest and accountable. The camera doesn't lie about what did or didn't happen, and we don't want to be the one who can't seem to either be honest or evaluate ourselves correctly. We won't last long that way.
- Next, every officiating position on the field has its respective position specialist. Most of them are current or retired NFL officials. This person looks at each position with an even higher level of scrutiny and specificity. While I may give myself a grade of "correct call" on a certain play, the specialist may disagree and change that positive grade to a negative one, or vice versa.
- We also have several people in the football office watching each game on a half-dozen screens at the same time. They are mostly there for collaborative replay purposes, but they are watching for any officiating issues that may need to be revisited later.

- Lastly, our supervisor weighs in on the final grading. I have to admit, I find it very impressive the amount of game film our supervisor consumes from Saturday morning to late Sunday evening. He's not just watching one game at a time—he's watching all of them.

When we receive our grades, we go back through the game film again to watch the specific plays in which the conference made grades or comments. Then, we repeat the cycle of texts, calls, and Zoom meetings to make sure everyone agrees on the things we're doing right and the areas where we need to improve for the next game.

After we go through our grades, we consider the previous week's game to be over, and on Wednesday and Thursday, it's time to move on to the next week's game. These are preparation days, and I use them to put myself in a position where, if at all possible, nothing will surprise me or catch me off guard in the upcoming Saturday's game.

For my preparation, each team in our crew's upcoming game gets their own day of review. Since one of my main officiating responsibilities is offensive line play, I spend a couple of hours watching each team's previous one or two games, wearing out the play and rewind buttons on the remote control, watching for specific things on each play. What did the left tackle do? When a defender beats a lineman, what does the lineman do to recover? How did that defensive lineman end up on the ground? What is the tight end doing when he double-teams a defender with the tackle? I go through every play like this, sometimes reaching out to other officials for their opinions about certain blocking techniques.

I watch every punt play. I make notes on formations teams use in their offense and what kinds of plays they're most likely to run out of their formations. I pay attention to tendencies, trying to identify what it means when a team sends a player in motion or how different alignments can impact which way a team will run the ball. By Saturday, I've probably watched more game film on a team than even their opponent has. After two days of this, I have a good foundation of what each team will do based on their alignment, which makes it much easier for me to be sure I'm in the right position and watching for the right things during each play on Saturday.

The last bit of preparation is our weekly training film. By Thursday morning, our supervisor sends us about a dozen plays to review, along with his commentary on each one. Some plays feature good officiating work in complicated circumstances that he wants to recognize and reinforce. Others focus on an area for potential improvement. And there are always a few plays that include something from another conference or the NFL that he believes we could benefit from. This film helps us to home in on important points of emphasis for the following week, and it's just one more way for us to make sure we're all on the same page.

Friday is a travel day for most of us, although as much as conferences have expanded geographically, I sometimes depart on Thursday to make sure I avoid any travel issues when I need to go across the country. When everyone arrives at the hotel by late Friday afternoon, there's still work to be done.

First and foremost, did everyone arrive safely? Sometimes a travel delay or other event, like an illness, family emergency, or work issue, can prevent the entire crew from arriving on time (or, in rare cases, from arriving at all). If that happens, we need to adjust quickly. Sometimes this means adjusting our meeting schedule, but if they're not going to make the game at all, we have to either find a replacement on short notice or plan on how we'll work with one less crew member.

Once the crew assembles on Friday night, we all have dinner together. This is a great time to reconnect, settle our minds, and shift our focus to what's coming on game day. We've been communicating throughout the week, but being face-to-face around a table in the same room is important as we prepare to take the field on Saturday.

Most of our games in the SEC kick off at noon Eastern Time, so most of the time, we do all our pregame work Friday night back at the hotel. We start with a brief review of last week's game. By this point, all of us have reviewed our grades and talked during the week, so this is one last step in ensuring everyone is on the same page. Then we watch the training tape that our supervisor sent earlier in the week, and even though I've already watched it, a second viewing always helps. I keep a file of my notes on these training tapes over the course of the season, and typically, trends develop—recurring issues that need to be addressed or points our supervisor is putting particular emphasis on. The faster I can pick up on these, the more I can improve my officiating.

After reviewing the training film, we move on to the rules test we received earlier in the week. The more we go through these example scenarios and their outcomes, the better we are. We'll challenge each other with as many "what if" questions as we can think of, and sometimes we'll come across a test question that forces us to dig deep into the rules to double-check what we know is the right answer. The power of a crew figuring it out together is exponentially greater than one of us struggling with it alone.

Next comes the scouting report. One or two members of the crew will present how they believe each of the teams operates, which includes featured players and special formations that we need to anticipate prior to seeing them on the field. We've done this during the week on an individual basis, but this gives us the chance to discuss as a group how we're going to officiate these two teams in specific situations and to share insights that others may not have observed.

Finally, Saturday arrives. Game day. We're required to be at the stadium a minimum of two and a half hours before kickoff. During this time, the referee and the umpire meet with each head coach separately. Typically, this is a very short conversation. The referee introduces himself and asks the coach if he has anything he wants to discuss. The coach usually says no, and the meeting is over. But now and then, it goes a little longer. Once, a coach brought out a whiteboard and showed us ten predrawn plays. Our referee acknowledged them and thanked the coach, not wanting to waste the coach's limited pregame time with his team. The coach said, "Hold on," and he flipped over the whiteboard to show ten more exotic plays. He didn't run a single one of those plays during the game.

After meeting with the coaches, the referee will attend a meeting with representatives from both schools, television production, stadium personnel, a meteorologist, and security. Normally games aren't impacted by issues like weather or security threats, but these meetings are still an important element of our preparation. I worked a game in 2016 that was delayed for hours by Hurricane Matthew. In 2022, we had a nearly three-hour delay at Texas A&M for lightning. I worked another game in 2021 at Tennessee where we had to delay the game for eighteen minutes because fans began throwing seemingly everything they could find onto the field when they disagreed with the result of a replay review—water bottles, tiny liquor bottles, mustard bottles, and even a golf ball. (Who brings a golf ball to a football game?) When moments like these come up, we have to have a plan in place, and that plan can vary based on the stadium and the situation.

The last thing we do is have some type of prayer, devotional, or—at the very least—a brief moment of calm shared as a crew before we head out into the organized chaos of the football field. We get our minds focused, knowing that there is nothing that will happen on that field that we can't handle. We know we've put in the work over the course of the offseason and every day of the week leading up to this moment, and we know that it's within our ability to officiate a fair contest between the two teams.

We prepare for well over six months to properly officiate a football game for three and a half hours. The expectations are sky-high. And we prepare so that we can rise to meet them.

What does your preparation look like? Think of a high-pressure situation you've faced in your life or career. How well do you feel you prepared for it? What could you have done better? Who are your "crewmates"? Whom can you call on to support you in important moments and help you prepare for them? What routines could you put in place for your preparation to make sure you achieve the result you're working for, every time? What are the disciplines you can adopt so that you're not just getting it right, but you're ensuring you can't get it wrong?

CHAPTER 9

COMMUNICATION

THE LACK OF solid communication is at the root of so many problems, issues, and mistakes. When something goes wrong, you can almost always trace it back to somebody not telling something to somebody else, or their message was misunderstood, misinterpreted, or misheard. We live in a world where, despite the countless methods of communication we have at our fingertips, it seems easier than ever to miscommunicate. Very few things in our work or life will set us up for success better than solid communication.

The same is true in football. If I'm communicating well with my crew over the course of each season, each week, and each game, we'll almost definitely succeed. And if I'm not . . . well, that's where mistakes can start creeping in that might show up on SportsCenter, and no official ever wants to show up on SportsCenter.

In football and in life, communication matters. In this chapter, I'm going to share the three elements of communication that have been most impactful for me in my career. I call them The Three

Cs of Communication. I know these matter in officiating, but I also believe they matter in life, both personal and professional, and that no matter what kind of work we do, we can all benefit from exercising them in our careers.

Communicating with Courage

The other day, I had to have an uncomfortable conversation with a family member. They were making an intentional choice to be a poor communicator about an important issue, and I felt like it was something we needed to address head-on.

I thought about how best to reach out to them. Should I send a text? No, not a good idea; texts can be so easily misinterpreted that I might make things worse. Email wouldn't be any better. I know myself well enough to know how I communicate in email. I spell things out, list out all the facts, and the next thing I know I've typed out an email that's longer than my arm and makes the reader feel attacked. They would respond with defensiveness, and we would be in a worse situation than we were in to begin with.

I knew what I needed to do. I needed to call them on the phone. I didn't want to. It didn't sound fun, or nearly as quick and easy as sending a text or email. But my goal was to make things better in the family situation, and I could see that doing so would take some courage. It would take me being willing to step into some discomfort and take a risk, knowing that the potential reward would be worth it.

When I see a foul on the football field, it takes courage to stop the game, every single time. Would it be easier to keep my flag in my pocket when I observe a holding foul that impacts the play? Sure it would. I could continue going about my business, and no eyes would be on me. But doing my job well requires that on every single play, I have the courage to stay true to what I observe on the field and uphold the standards I have set for myself. If that requires me to stop the game, look my referee in the eye, and say, "I've got a holding foul on number 87 of the offense, ten-yard penalty, repeat second down," then that's what I have to do. Then we relay that information to the coach on the sideline. It's not a conversation we look forward to because we know the response is going to be one of disapproval, but it is what needs to be done. Avoiding it is not the answer.

One of the reasons I love football is because all 180 or more plays over the course of a game are opportunities for somebody to step up. Somebody has to call the false start before the ball is even snapped. When there's a super-tight play with a receiver going to the ground while trying to catch the ball, somebody has to step up and have the courage to say whether the pass was complete or incomplete. Somebody has to determine whether the block that sprung the running back for the eighty-yard touchdown run was legal, or if the entire play has to be brought back because it was a holding foul. Somebody has to have the courage to call a targeting foul that they believe they observed, knowing that their call will be reviewed by instant replay and could be overturned. Someone has to stop the game with eight seconds left on the clock with the score tied because there should be ten seconds remaining. And if you think that doesn't matter, how many times have you seen a team win by kicking a field goal with two seconds left? It happens. It matters. One hundred eighty times a game, we have to have the courage to say the hard thing when necessary. How many times are you at work, home, or somewhere else and you see something that you know isn't quite right? Do you choose to address it or pretend you didn't see it?

When we go to the sideline and explain a situation, we have the head coach (and possibly multiple assistants) following us up and down the sideline, ready to bark at us over anything they find to be unfair in their eyes. We have a stadium full of fans watching our every move. We have cameras following us, ready to turn us into a meme if we make one wrong move or a bad call that impacts the game. As officials, we have to know whether we have the courage to deal with all of it. Are we going to let it break us down, or are we going to rise above it? Are we going to run from it, or face it head-on?

The reality is, if I'm not ready to communicate with courage, everyone suffers. I could get my crew in trouble. I could be suspended or not brought back the next season if my error was egregious enough. I have the potential to unfairly disadvantage one team over the other, which is unfair to the schools, coaches, players, and fans. If my error has a material impact on the game, it could result in a team losing a game, causing them to receive a lower-profile bowl game at the end of the season, or possibly missing out on a bowl game altogether. That equates to millions of dollars for that school that I cost them. It could be the difference between a team having a winning or losing record. A coach or entire staff could lose their jobs, displacing thirty people and their families. And all because I didn't have the courage to do the right thing. I have less than two seconds to identify, mentally process, and decide. It takes courage to take that on.

There's nowhere to hide in football officiating. The risk is there, and it's real. If I'm not willing to step up and make the call that needs to be made, there are two hundred people who would be happy to come take my place and make that call.

Making a choice that doesn't require courage might seem easier, but if you want to succeed in any role—as an official, spouse, parent, or business leader—you need to be courageous in your communication to get there.

Communicating with Clarity

On October 21, 2023, we were in our pregame meeting before a game in Columbia, Missouri, between the South Carolina Gamecocks and the Missouri Tigers. Someone suggested that we use more hand signals during the game to allow us to enforce penalties faster. I knew right away what we'd be doing if we implemented this idea: cutting corners on communication for the sake of speed. I made it known that I disagreed, but others wanted to try it. So, we did.

With about thirteen minutes left in the second quarter, South Carolina had the ball at the Missouri forty-three-yard line. Spencer Rattler, South Carolina's quarterback, dropped back to pass, and after not finding an open receiver, he ran for two yards up the middle. During the play, South Carolina center Nick Gargiulo made a solid block on Missouri defensive tackle Jayden Jernigan. Gargiulo laid on top of Jernigan a bit too long after the play was over, though, and Jernigan didn't care for it. He let Gargiulo know, and there was some pushing and shoving and some "friendly" conversation after the play. I moved in between them to break it up and sent the players back to their respective huddles. No harm, no foul.

One of my on-field duties was to run to where the play ended, which was the middle of the field at the Missouri forty-two-yard line. I could tell that I had missed something while breaking up the skirmish, so I started asking questions. I asked another official, "What was the result of the play?"

"Running play to this spot," he responded.

Great, I thought. I went to put the ball down. Then, my colleague approached me. "There was a foul on the play," he said.

"What kind of foul?" I asked, with a hint of sarcasm in my tone as I tried to fight off my sudden annoyance.

"Holding," he replied.

Okay, holding. I left the spot where the play had ended, and I went back to the previous spot so I could walk off ten yards against the offense for holding.

"No!" he said. "It's against the defense!"

Then I blew a gasket. "That would have been good to know in the beginning!"

Let me tell you, the second I took my foot off the correct place on the field, the data immediately dumped from my brain. I was stuck between two different fouls with opposite enforcements in opposite directions, and I had completely lost my spot on the field. I was not happy.

My referee, realizing there was a delay, asked me, "Didn't you hear my announcement?"

"Hell no, I didn't hear your announcement!" I yelled, my blood pressure escalating. "I was busy breaking up a fight!"

Everything broke down because other officials on the crew tried to use hand signals to administer a penalty for a foul I didn't know had occurred. Typically, we share this information verbally, either by using on-field radio devices that each of us carries or by coming together face-to-face. Spectators may notice that all of us have earpieces and microphones. We abandoned that in favor of hand signals, we didn't communicate with clarity, and it almost cost us.

Saying what needs to be said is one thing. But the second half of communication—the more important half—is making sure the person on the other end has received the message. The single most difficult place to hear a referee's announcement of a penalty is on the field. The speakers are pointed up toward the stands, not toward us. As the guy whose job it was to enforce the penalty, I need to know what happened more than just about anybody else in the stadium. But the message wasn't given in a way that I could receive it, and when someone had the opportunity to communicate it to me directly, they did so in a manner that lacked clarity. Tiny things can become big problems.

In officiating, clarity is everything. We have to make sure we're on the same page at all times, and to do that, we have to make sure everything we say is crystal clear. We have to speak the same language, and whenever we say anything, we have to make sure it's as clear as possible so the other person receives all the information we're trying to convey.

We have such limited time to do this on the football field that we have to be intentional with our words. If I call a holding penalty, it's not going to help my referee if I report to him, "Well, I saw one guy grab the other guy's jersey when the guy with the ball was running away. The guy on defense was number 90, and the offensive guy is that one over there, see? The one with the grass stuck in his face mask?" No, I know exactly what information I need to convey to my referee, and I know exactly how he needs to receive it: "Holding, on the offense, number 65, ten-yard penalty, repeat second down." I'm quick, I'm clear, and the game moves on without a hitch.

It's not just with other members of my officiating crew, though. When I'm communicating with a coach, I have to remember whom I'm talking to. If I want the coach to receive my message in the way I'm trying to communicate it, I have to communicate in a way he'll be able to receive it.

If I tell a coach, "Hey, your left tackle is holding," he might get defensive right off the bat. But if I try to speak in coaching language and say, "Hey, your left tackle has hands outside the frame, and he's got a bad foundation with his feet," he'll know exactly what I'm talking about because he sees it, too. I'm able to communicate clearly with him because I'm aware of who he is and how he'll best receive what I have to say. I'm speaking his language.

Clarity matters in all communication—in football and in life—and one of the most important elements of clear communication is remembering whom you're talking to. Know your audience. What do they need to hear? How do they need to hear it? What will get in the way of them receiving the message you're trying to convey? The next time you are in a business meeting with a customer or prospect, pay attention to the words you use. Are you speaking in your own company's language, using terms and acronyms that are familiar to you but sound like a foreign language to the person on the other side of the table? I see it all the time, and then we wonder why the other person doesn't engage further or even understand our message.

Without communication, we wouldn't last through two plays on a football field. And no matter how many fancy hand signals we might try, our communication is worthless without clarity.

Communicating with Commitment

No one is successful by themselves.

Our officiating crew comprises ten officials every Saturday—eight of us on the field and two in the replay booth. If even one of us isn't fully committed to what we need to accomplish together, it's game over. We'll all fail. To succeed, we *need* each other.

We operate under the philosophy that we all succeed together, and we all fail together. We're each committed to the success of the crew as a whole and to the success of each member of that crew. That requires us to be all-in, all the time.

Our commitment to each other drives the way we communicate. The game of football moves so fast that if at any point we're not communicating with commitment to each other, we could miss something crucial and let the rest of the crew down. We have to be committed at all times to giving our crewmates all the information they need to be successful and standing by each other to make sure that even in the most complicated situation, we get it right.

Every game, I have to operate from the understanding that what I do isn't just about me—it impacts the success or failure of the other people on my crew. And these aren't just random people assigned to the same game that I was. These are my friends, my brothers, the people I care deeply about as human beings. If I hold back in a game and we fail because of it, I'll make all of us look bad. If we're in a study session and I notice something that I don't point out, I'm not helping to set us up for success as a group. I do my job so that others are able to do their job.

This kind of communication takes trust. We have to display the same commitment to each other's success in the offseason and during the week, when we're not in the heat of battle on the football field, that we do every Saturday. We build solid bonds. We display through our actions and communications that we're all committed to each other. When game time comes, all of that allows us to step onto the field with no pretense. We understand that we're all in this together, and no matter what gets said (or how it gets said), we know that it's all for the good of our crew.

In any given situation on the football field, we have about two seconds to mentally calculate the right decision. We know that we'll have the chance to process through that situation together in a much more relaxed environment after the game and during the week to come, but in the moment, everyone just needs the answer. Sometimes we are very direct with each other on the field. In fact, if anyone listened to our conversations on the field, they might not always walk away thinking we are close friends off the field. But that directness, even bluntness at times, comes from our commitment and accountability to each other's success. We need the answer as quickly as possible, and if we're each committed to that goal in the moment, that's all that matters.

Sometimes communicating out of this commitment is hard—even scary. All of us officials are human. We don't have the ability to magically watch a replay in our heads when we're not one hundred percent certain about something. So, the commitment we make to each other is to always make the best decision we can with the information we have and to communicate that decision with honesty, even if it means that we tell another official their ruling is wrong. We are committed to getting it right for the crew and the game.

In 2021, during a game between Ole Miss and Tennessee, there was a play where the Ole Miss quarterback had been wrapped up and was being driven back by multiple Tennessee defenders. All of a sudden, the ball squirted out, and Tennessee picked it up and ran it back for a touchdown. It was a huge play, and needless to say, the stadium was in complete pandemonium. Had forward progress been stopped? Should this have been a turnover and a touchdown for Tennessee, or should Ole Miss keep the ball?

To get it right, we needed full commitment to each other at that moment. We gathered quickly as a crew. Remembering a similar situation that had happened in a game the previous season, I said, "Guys, we don't do cheap turnovers, and we don't do cheap scores."

"We need to mark him down because his forward progress had stopped," said one of my colleagues. "Not a fumble."

Our referee said, "Okay." And that's what we did. A complicated problem solved simply, quickly, and with accountability to each other as a group. There was risk involved in being the person who spoke up, who put their neck on the line to help get the call right, but none of us hesitated. In a couple of seconds, three of us contributed to the decision, and everyone else agreed. After the game, when we were talking through that play again, our evaluator said to us, "Guys, you did exactly the right thing. That situation wasn't reviewable. You were the only ones who could've gotten to the right outcome, and you did."

Communicating with commitment means being accountable to the people on your team. It takes courage because sometimes you might be wrong. But you have to be willing to put yourself on the line on behalf of the people around you, and you need them to do the same thing for you.

Anyone who gets into officiating of any kind understands that at the end of the game, somebody's going to be unhappy. It doesn't matter if you're officiating the Super Bowl, umpiring a Little League game, or judging a dog show, if you're in a position of being the adjudicator of a ruling, someone is going to disagree with your decision. Sometimes, *everybody* is going to disagree with your decision. It's just part of the gig.

But communication is the key that can help any one of us break free of the pressure that brings. If we communicate with commitment to each other, we will know we are not alone, that we're all in it together. If we communicate with clarity, we'll know that nothing is getting lost in translation—that whatever decision we reach, we'll have reached it with all the facts in front of us. If we communicate with courage, then we'll know we left it all out on the field, no matter how intimidating it might have felt to do so.

It matters in football, and it matters in life. As I said at the start of this chapter, the lack of communication is the root of so many problems. But solid communication—with courage, clarity, and commitment—lays a foundation of trust. It sets you up for success, for thriving collaboration, and for the chance to flourish as a team and as individuals.

Think about what goes into the communication you have with others you care about or who are mutual stakeholders.

Think about a time when you communicated with courage. What was the result? How did your courage help drive you forward in the situation? What situations in your life require courageous communication from you right now?

Think about a time you could have used more clarity in your communication. What could you do differently in the future to make sure your message is clear? To whom are you committed? What does it look like to communicate with them in light of that commitment?

CHAPTER 10

PATIENCE

IN THE MIDDLE of what had been a normal prep week in one of my seasons working in the MAC, I got a phone call from my referee. One of the teams in our upcoming game was Temple, and apparently, their coach was still heated over something that had happened during their previous game.

Temple had played Ohio University in a midweek game, and the game was close. Temple had a slight lead. Ohio had the ball on their own twenty-two-yard line with time winding down, and they needed a miracle to avoid a loss. Then, they got one: a fifty-yard pass to set up a touchdown a few plays later to win the game. There was just one problem. It appeared that one of Ohio's linemen had held Temple's linebacker, who could have potentially made a tackle to hold Ohio U to an eight-yard gain rather than a fifty-yard gain. But at the end of the play, there were no flags on the field. It was a potential missed holding foul, and it essentially won the game.

Understandably, the Temple coach was irate on the sideline. His anger didn't fade over the course of the week. If anything, it seemed to grow. He had called our supervisor that same night of the game to complain about the call, and he shared his belief that we were going to look for any opportunity we could find to screw him over in the next game, which was also scheduled to be a midweek matchup. He called again on Friday, then again on Monday, saying all the same things. It didn't matter that it was a different crew. He was convinced that anyone wearing a black-and-white striped shirt was out to get him.

All of this meant one thing for us: we were about to walk into a hornet's nest.

Game time arrived. On the third play of the game, Temple threw a long pass down the sideline that was caught by their receiver. I was there to rule on the sideline play, and I had a clear angle to see the receiver get one foot down in bounds before falling out of bounds, which is all you need in college football for a pass to be complete. It was a tight catch, but in my eyes, there were clearly a couple of blades of green grass between the receiver's foot and the sideline. I ruled the pass complete, got the ball back from the receiver—and immediately got buzzed by replay. The play was going to be reviewed to make sure I got the call right.

I have only one in-game photo hanging in my office at home. It's not me standing next to Nick Saban, or with my crew at the SEC championship, or even on the field in my first-ever college game. It's me standing like a statue in front of the head coach of the Temple Owls, who is shoving his finger into my chest, screaming in my face, spit flying from out of his mouth. "I f––g knew it!" he yelled. "I knew you guys were gonna screw me over the first chance you got! I can't believe this!"

The worst thing I possibly could have done in that situation would have been to try to argue with the coach. It's our job as officials to be impartial, to keep the game *fair*. If I'd said something back, then the coach would have called my supervisor after the game and said, "Hey, Garner tried to screw me over and then told me to shut my mouth and not worry about it." It wouldn't have helped my case if there was game film of me having a heated argument with the coach. I wasn't the one who called for the replay. My call on the field was in favor of Temple! But none of that mattered in the moment. My only defense was standing there with my mouth closed, patiently allowing this coach to voice his grievance.

As we say in the world of officiating, silence can't be misquoted. I just had to take a breath, listen, and be patient.

Of course, replay took a look and quickly confirmed my call. The catch stood. But that didn't stop this coach. He spent the rest of the game tearing into every official who dared enter his presence, calling several of us every name in the book (including several I won't include in *this* book).

What we didn't know at the time was that the television broadcast was picking up almost every word he said to us. It was a midweek game on national TV. During our game, it just so happened that ESPN was covering the Jerry Sandusky scandal at Penn State, which was coming to light in real time. ESPN was showing a split screen, our game on one side and news coverage from Happy Valley on the other. College football was getting a major black eye from the incidents unfolding at Penn State, and a Division I coach losing his composure at an officiating crew over minor perceived slights wasn't helping.

When I came back out onto the field for the second half, Temple's coach was gone. When I say "gone," I am telling you that I was looking for him and couldn't find him anywhere on the sideline. It was apparent that someone had heard what he was saying during the TV broadcast—using just about every four-letter word in the book—and told him he was done for the night.

Dealing with coaches is part of being an official at any level of football. In Division I, we're under a microscope every time we walk onto the field. There's game film from many different angles of everything we do. If I hadn't been able to exercise patience with Temple's coach, I easily could have fallen into the trap of trying to debate the situation with him, then I would have gotten a call on Tuesday from my supervisor asking me to explain why he's spent the last half hour watching me shove *my* finger into the chest of a coach whose game I was supposed to be officiating impartially.

I've seen it happen. I've seen officials try to have that conversation with coaches, get caught up in their own emotions, go a step too far, and get caught on camera. They get caught in the trap, and when they do, that season tends to be their last. They disappear.

Football officials aren't unemotional robots. It doesn't feel good when we've worked so hard to prepare, to make sure the game is fair to both teams, to be as impartial as possible, and to do our best to get every call right, only to have a coach yell in our face and tell us we're horrible and that we're trying to screw over his team. We're human. We have feelings, just like everyone else.

That's why patience matters so, so much in what we do. We have to be able to pause, take a breath, remember what's important in that moment, and keep our composure. If one of us loses our patience with a coach once, that could be all it takes to end our career.

Six Seconds of Patience

Patience is key to everything we do as college football officials. It matters dealing with coaches on the sideline between plays. It matters just as much when we're on the field in the middle of the action. As crazy as it sounds, if we're not patient on each play—for the thirty seconds before the play, and for the entire six seconds the play lasts—we could make a mistake that impacts the outcome of the game.

During a game between Alabama and Texas in 2023, Alabama trailed in the fourth quarter and had the ball deep in their own territory. It was second down and ten, and Alabama needed to gain a lot of yards fast. The energy was flowing through the stadium, and my own adrenaline was pumping. It was a critical moment in the game.

Jalen Milroe, Alabama's quarterback, dropped back to pass. Immediately, I saw Alabama's left tackle holding on for dear life as he got absolutely dominated by Texas's defensive end. The left tackle was holding, literally, in every sense of the word. We always say to each other that to make a holding call, you want the grandma sitting in the top row of the stadium to see it and know that it's holding. That's exactly what I had. She could see this one.

As Alabama's tackle took the Texas defensive end to the ground, I pulled out my penalty flag and wound up to throw it like a major league pitcher throwing a fastball. There was just one problem—in one final, heroic effort, the defender lunged at Milroe and brought him down for a sack.

This brought up several questions at once, all related to our officiating philosophies. Did Alabama's tackle commit a textbook holding foul? Absolutely. But did the hold have any impact on the play? The defender he was blocking sacked the quarterback, so obviously not. The defense was able to successfully complete their assignment. Would Texas accept a holding penalty, allowing Alabama to replay second down, when their defender had just brought the quarterback down for a big loss *plus* a loss of down? Not a chance.

And these questions brought me to the biggest question: If I threw my flag in that moment, would I be doing anything other than disrupting the flow of the game for no reason at all?

I put my flag away.

The right camera angle on the TV broadcast shows me there, my arm cocked back like a pitcher, ready to throw my flag. And then, as the defender completes the sack, I very slyly lower the flag and hide it in my pocket. (The audio also captures the broadcasters momentarily losing their minds, questioning why I wouldn't call such an obvious holding foul.)

If I'd exercised a bit more patience, waiting for the play to fully unfold, I wouldn't have gotten caught having to unpull the trigger. I knew that if the defender completed the sack, calling the penalty would have been the wrong thing to do. But I didn't wait. All I needed was just a few more *seconds* of patience, and I wouldn't have looked like I was second-guessing myself in front of a national television audience.

It sounds counterintuitive, but officiating live game action takes a tremendous amount of patience even while operating at high speed. Plays take an average of about six seconds, but within those six seconds, we need patience to see how a play develops, how it ends, and all the little details in between that can't be missed if we want to manage the game correctly.

We have to do it nearly two hundred times per game. And for every single one of those times, we have to be disciplined enough to exercise patience. If I don't follow my presnap routine before every play, I'll get my reads wrong and miss something that's going to impact that play's outcome. If I don't observe the play all the way through to its completion, I might make an assumption that leads me to make a call prematurely, or I won't watch the play as closely as I should. These are incredible athletes we're watching. Just because a pass looks uncatchable to me doesn't mean the wide receiver streaking down the field won't make an amazing play. Just because it seems like the defensive end is getting held by the tackle doesn't mean he won't still find a way to sack the quarterback.

On the football field, we have to practice short bursts of intense patience. The time between our presnap reads and the end of the play may be only thirty seconds or so, but if we're not extremely disciplined during that time to not get ahead of ourselves, everything is thrown off. We can't make assumptions. We can't move on from one play just because we're ready for the next one.

We have to be present, in the moment, exactly where we are, every second of the game.

Patience on the Journey

One of the best things I ever did for my officiating career was giving myself time.

When I first got into Division III, I had achieved my primary goal as an official. I wanted to be able to say I had officiated college football—even working one junior college game would have given me that. Getting to work a full D-III schedule? I was happy as a clam. It was great!

But as I started getting a little deeper into the pool, especially as I got to know some people who worked in higher divisions, I started imagining more for myself. I was thirty-two (which is young for a college official), in the best shape of my life, and working at a high level where I was. I felt like it wasn't a stretch to say that I had as good a chance as anyone working D-III to make it to the next level. The timing was right. All the puzzle pieces were there. What does it take to put a puzzle together? Time and patience.

I knew beyond any doubt that it was going to take patience. I felt like I had a chance to make a run at higher levels of officiating, but it wasn't going to happen overnight.

My second year in Division III, I had a solid season, especially for a newer official. I worked a full schedule, graded out well, and earned the trust of the other officials on my crew. I was doing all the right things. Even so, it guaranteed nothing.

At the end of the season, I got a phone call from my referee. "I want to tell you two things," he said. "First, you had a great year, and you really helped the crew have a great year. I was just informed that our crew has been awarded a playoff game, and you've been an integral part of the team. We wouldn't be here without you.

"The second thing I want to tell you is that you're not going. I shared with our supervisor that you were every bit as much a part of our success as any of the rest of us and that it would be wrong to leave you behind. But he believes that you don't have enough experience to work a playoff game."

I was disappointed, but being just two years in, I took it fairly well, certainly better than I would have in my fifth year. But that moment demonstrated to me how important patience would be to me if I was going to achieve my goals as an official. At that moment, I had two choices. It would've been very easy to be angry about it, but what would that have solved? I chose the second option and took that moment as a challenge to demonstrate how hard I was willing to work, how good an official I could be, and how much time I was willing to dedicate to getting better. I decided to be patient.

I knew that, realistically, I was going to have to work at least five years in D-III before I had a chance of moving up. So, I gave myself time and learned to be patient with the process. I decided I was going to work like crazy for the next three years and not spend time worrying about things I couldn't control. I gave myself grace to work hard for five years in D-III, to go to camps and clinics, learn, grow, build relationships, and let them flourish.

At the end of those five years, I knew I had done everything I possibly could have done. I left it all on the field. Not long after, I got the phone call. It was my time.

End-to-end, it took me about ten years to get from day one of officiating in high school to joining a D-I crew full-time. Ten years is not a short amount of time, but in the officiating world, that's actually pretty fast. Some incredibly hardworking, deserving officials have to wait fifteen to twenty years to get their shot, some longer, and some never make it at all.

It takes patience to keep working toward a goal when you know that goal is at least ten years away. You have to be willing to give yourself grace, to understand that there will be disappointments along the way, and to acknowledge that ten years could easily turn into something more. You have to come to grips with the fact that nothing is guaranteed—that you can work as hard as anybody, be as good as anybody, and still get passed over, no matter how deserving you might be.

I've seen it happen with some of the most talented officials I know. For Jay Brown, it was more than twenty years before he joined the SEC. He showed a level of dedication, work ethic, and patience that's several levels above anything I ever had to do. For some others—like Jonathan Shelton, whom I still consider the best football official I know—that phone call to go to the next level never comes.

The patience it takes to keep grinding, to keep putting in the work day after day to be the best that you can be in the midst of that uncertainty, is something any of us could benefit from in many parts of our lives. I've learned so much from my own experiences navigating my football career. But looking at some of the other officials I know who have had to show even higher levels of patience inspires me in ways that stretch far beyond football.

Bottom line: be where your feet are. I never had any guarantee that I'd end up officiating in both the Big Ten and SEC. A lot of things needed to break my way, and I needed a lot of help from a lot of people. But if I hadn't committed myself to the daily grind, to being present right where I was, and to being the best version of myself I could be, I never would have made it.

Patience helped get me to where I am today—in football and in life.

I would ask this of anyone who is pressing hard to get to another level: examine your patience. What's a situation in your life right now that requires patience? How are you doing in that situation? Is there something you can do differently to make sure you're focusing on the things you can control? Who has shown patience in a way you could learn from? What attitudes or practices do you see in their life that you could implement in your own life?

Is there an area of your life where you need to give yourself more grace? More time? More patience? I believe you will find that the more you can take a breath and be grateful for what you have accomplished and give everything to your current situation, the faster the next potential level will come.

CHAPTER 11

EMBRACE THE GRIND

WHENEVER I HEAR someone say they are number one in something, it always makes me raise my eyebrows.

I have worked as a sales leader in the corporate world for a long time, and when I interview sales candidates, they all somehow seem to be the number-one salesperson in their company, region, or local office. I've experienced the same thing in the college football world. Commissioners from nearly every conference like to claim that they have the best officials in the country. But here's the truth: the universal laws of physics don't allow everyone to be number one at the same time. So, who's right?

It doesn't matter. Because no matter the answer to that question, that answer is always in the past.

Even when there is a way to prove who's the best, that title only refers to a singular point in time. It could change at literally any moment. If I get it in my head that I'm the best in my corporate job because I was the top salesperson last year, I scored 100 percent on the rules exam in football, I got a good score on their weekly quiz, or I graded well in last week's game, I'm pointing at something that happened in the past. When my supervisor gets a call from a coach on Sunday about a call I missed, I doubt very seriously my supervisor tells him, "Well, coach, I see your point, but Chris did get 100 percent on the test two months ago." That's ancient history.

In officiating and in life, there is something called The Grind. If you want to be great, you owe The Grind. It is always coming to collect its debt. It's coming every day. The Grind doesn't care if you're tired, if you had a bad day, or whether or not you want to pay up. We're not promised success, but if you want to achieve success, The Grind is the path you must travel to get there.

I used to work out with another SEC official during the summer. He didn't like to run, and when we would work out together, he never wanted to push himself any harder than he had to. When I asked him if he could do one more lap, push himself for just a few more minutes, he'd turn me down. But then, in the same conversation, he'd complain about the way his games were grading out, how much he didn't like his position coach, and not getting assigned to a bowl again.

My response would always be the same. When he said he didn't want to run farther or faster, I'd tell him, "Don't worry. I'm sure several other guys who work your same position are still running. And don't worry about your bowl assignment being lonely because it will get filled by someone who wants it more."

And it did. His bowl assignment and eventually his spot in the SEC were both filled by someone else. That official isn't in the SEC anymore. He didn't want to pay into The Grind.

In officiating and in life, there is something called The Standard. I was reminded of this by University of Nebraska football coach Matt Rhule. The Standard is not something that we should aspire to—it is the absolute minimum acceptable level to perform at. When I was in the military, I would hear senior leaders refer to the American flag that we carried as The Standard. I never really knew why they called it that, so I researched it. The meaning of the word "standard" can be traced back to the action of planting a flag for military purposes, a way of emphatically indicating a refusal to retreat backward from that point. It's derived from an ancient German word *standort*, meaning "to stand hard."

On an officiating crew, someone has to be responsible for setting The Standard. Traditionally, it's the referee, who then has to hold the crew accountable to it. If eight crew members all pay into The Grind, then they can hold themselves and each other to The Standard.

As an official, if you're not willing to meet The Standard and push it forward even further, then it's time to make a career decision. There are too many people coming for you, thousands of other officials working to take your spot. They are younger, faster, better with technology, and hungry to advance. Not to mention all the fans, coaches, and media who would love to point a finger in your direction.

Everything we do is a choice. If my crewmates can't trust me to study the rule book, master the new rule changes, work every practice quiz and exam inside and out, go to the gym, eat right, and show up in August in shape and ready to go, how are they going to trust me on Saturday afternoon? That's what The Grind demands. That's The Standard. May, June, and July are easy. But what about when we get to week ten of the season? Are we still working just as hard, or are we coasting? No one, absolutely no one, is allowed to coast.

This is what The Standard demands in officiating. But it exists in life, too. If you want to be great, to accomplish anything significant, you have to be willing to pay into The Grind, live up to The Standard, and advance it forward. At the end of the day, you are the only one who looks in the mirror and knows whether you're doing the work. The results will play out in real life. Whatever those results are, you know if you prepared, and you know if you didn't. You know if you paid into The Grind, and you know if you didn't. You know if you upheld The Standard and tried to advance it, and you know if you didn't.

For those who don't want to do any of those things, you are average. You're doing what most everyone else does, the way most others do it, because it's easy. What is the cost of being average? Think about it. What is the cost to you personally? It affects the speed at which you grow, develop, and get compensated. What is the cost to those with whom you work, or your colleagues, stakeholders, subordinates, and, most importantly, the people in your family who are counting on you to *not* be average?

What did you do to be great today? If you didn't do anything, then you have lost a day. There is never a do-over for yesterday. You had it, and now it has passed. For most of us, we are on the backside of our careers, and we can see retirement or the day when we no longer do what we're doing now. Is that when you are going to wish you would've given more effort?

I have seen it a hundred times in football. "Next year, I'll study the rules harder." "Next year, I'll lose 10 pounds." "Next year, I'll be a better crewmate." In whatever it is you do, how many more years are you going to say that about yourself? For those of you who are on the front side of your career, the sooner you relentlessly pursue greatness, the more fulfilling your career becomes. Why are you waiting to be successful and to live to your fullest potential?

If you're worried about the cost of the hard work it takes to be better, wait until you see the cost of staying exactly where you are. Anybody can be average because that's the easy way. So, what separates you from average?

Georgia football coach Kirby Smart asks his team, "Can you

do the simple things better? How much are you willing to do the simple things better? You can't get bored with the simple things because your mastery of that is what makes you great." Doing the simple things better is what allows us to solve the more complex tasks.

I will end with this. I believe I have the secret of life figured out, and there are two parts to it. The first part is something many of us can do: identify opportunity. It can be anything from spotting someone who needs help opening a door, noticing that someone dropped their wallet or left their purse on top of their car, or observing someone at work struggle with a job-related task. Maybe you have an idea for a new business or invention. Maybe it's an investment idea. Perhaps you have always wanted to write a book and stand up in front of others and share it. For the most part, identifying opportunity is easy.

The second part is harder. How many of us actually do something about the opportunity? How many of us hold the door open, help others at work, pursue an investment, or act on a new business idea? How many of you have a book idea or have been told you need to write a book about your experiences but don't take the next step? Think about the experiences you have and the things you can do with them.

In his book *The Traveler's Gift*, Andy Andrews paints a picture of the end of your life. In this picture, you're walking through a warehouse-like structure on your way to wherever it is you believe you're going. The warehouse is full of containers. The ones on the right are full. The ones on the left are empty or incomplete. The full ones are your accomplishments. The empty ones are things you wish you would've done or started and didn't finish. The question Andrews says you need to ask yourself is how you can maximize the opportunities to be better than average, pay into The Grind, uphold The Standard, and master the simple things, while at the same time minimizing the unfinished business and areas where you fall below average.

The best people you ever meet are the people who have patience, pay into The Grind, and uphold and advance The Standard. They set an example every day. It doesn't matter what day it is, they set the example. It doesn't matter how hard the task is, they set an example. It doesn't matter what others are doing or the amount of peer pressure they experience, they set the example. Your job as a human being is to look for opportunities to set an example.

When someone is getting picked on, set an example and put an end to it. When someone wants to drive drunk, set an example and take their keys. When someone is in distress, be the one to help and set an example. When others see it, they will follow, and you will have made a difference in the world.

Everything is possible. Believing it is everything.

ACKNOWLEDGMENTS

This book is for all of those who have ever picked up a whistle or stood on a boundary line. For all of you who have had to stand there with a coach yelling at you because they want a ruling to go their way because they only see it through their lens. For the young adults who run up and down the floor of a girls' junior high basketball game while a forty-year-old parent hurls insults for everyone to hear. For anyone who's had the courage to come out of the bleachers of the little league game to help call balls and strikes—foul or fair, safe or out. For all of the track and field umpires, marshals, starters, and timekeepers who spend an entire day or weekend so that every participant can compete. For all those who officiated an under-ten youth soccer game in the rain, and anyone who worked an elementary-school-age flag football game for three dollars and a hotdog. For all of you who know that it's not about the money, but so the game can be played, and played as fairly as possible.

To every non-sports official, who, when finding out what I do in the fall, would ask me a dozen questions, and to every business associate who would introduce me in a meeting as the football official. You proved to me over and over that fans of the game are starving for insight into what we do and how we do it. Your persistence pushed me forward to share my passion with all of you.

There aren't enough pages to recognize the many people who have helped me navigate the officiating world. Anyone who has made it knows it's because of countless others who have helped along the way.

My wife, Anna, and my children, Hanna, Jonathan, and Olivia, all of you inspire me to be better every day. Don't ever stop following your dreams.

Special thanks to my mom. She always told me I could become whatever I wished in life.

Randy Felumlee, thank you for inviting me into your high school football world in Utica, Ohio. It literally saved my life.

Bill Leffler, you were absolutely the right man at the right time to teach me how to be a better human being as I figured out a pathway in life.

Kelly Miller, Doug Marston, and Tim Ginger. These are the three guys out of Newark, Ohio, who picked me back up every time I failed when I first learned how to officiate.

Doug Murphy, Dave Hankinson, Max Tharp, and Steve Harrington. You taught me how to work on Friday nights, and we loved every minute of it.

Rick Bueter, who invited me to my first college football rules meeting and helped me kick the door open to this opportunity.

Jonathan Shelton, I will never forget that you told me there is a difference between knowing the rules and knowing how to manage the game.

Everyone in the Ohio Association of Football Officials.

Norm Nelson, who during his time in the Big Ten always took time to help me while I was still dreaming about breaking into college football.

Dr. Larry Glass, who was the supervisor of officials in the

Division III Ohio Athletic Conference. He was the first to take a chance on me as a college official and eventually let me wear the white hat as a referee.

Phil Barnes, who brought me into the Division II Great Lakes Intercollegiate Athletic Conference as a referee.

Big Ten Supervisor of Officials, Bill Carollo and Bobb Waggoner, who brought me into the Mid-American and Big Ten and always listened to and mentored me.

Our Mid-American Conference crew: Greg Blum, Brian Bollinger, Grady Smith, Bob McElwee, John Hanneke, and Todd Boyd. It was a great run, and it continues to be.

Gary Arthur, NFL Super Bowl line judge: as my position coach in the Mid-American and Big Ten, you challenged me to chase perfection of the fundamentals. You also shared your philosophy of looking for the little explosions that can propel your career forward.

Former SEC Supervisor of Officials, Steve Shaw, who took a chance on a northern guy and brought me into the SEC.

Current SEC Supervisor of Officials, John McDaid, who is a great teacher and always surprises me with how well he knows the smallest details of everyone on his staff.

My center judge position coaches, Jon Bible and Butch Hannah. Both of you taught me the position and to work it to the best of my ability. You are both the best teachers I could've hoped to have. You always challenged me to be better tomorrow than I was yesterday.

My SEC Crewmates and football brothers: Marc Curles, Brent Sowell, Chris Conway, Randall Kizer, Chris Jamison, Wes Booker, Scott Vaughn, Ed Balbis, Matt Hollifield, Ron Turner, Kyle Olson, Marc Bovos, Albert Bryant, Chris Bikowski. Every football Saturday we stepped into the arena together and we came out together. No matter the circumstances, there wasn't anything we faced that we couldn't handle. Our officiating success on the field was only exceeded by our friendship off of it.

To every center judge in the SEC and Sun Belt, I have been chasing the excellence that all of you bring and hoping that I capture some measure of success along the way.

Russ Pulley, you challenged me early on to excel at rules knowledge, pushed me to be better, and encouraged me to never settle for average.

Jay Brown and Jason McArthur, you two have made it your life's work to help others in officiating know the rules. So many officials are better because of your help and insight on how the game is to be played.

Mike Boshers, we were two newbies working side by side and nailed it at the Mississippi State clinic to earn our way in to the next level.

Bill Failor, you were the best manager and leader I have ever had. You taught me the right way the first time on how to handle clients and develop others on the team.

Jon Gordon, thank you for sharing with me how I can accomplish writing my book and sharing positivity to more people.

To everyone at Streamline Books, Alex Demczak, Will Severns (aka Frank Spork), Donnel McLohon, and Andrew Blackburn. Your enthusiasm and support to help me finish this project is what got me to the starting line and helped me cross the finish line.

ABOUT THE AUTHOR

For the past twenty-five years, Chris Garner has led high-performing sales teams across the country while simultaneously officiating in one of college football's most prestigious conferences. His unique position—managing highly competitive teams on Saturdays while also leading driven sales professionals during the week—gives him an unmatched perspective on leadership, performance, and success.

Known for his ability to make split-second decisions under intense pressure, Garner shares his expertise through speaking engagements and leadership training, helping others apply the principles of elite sports officiating to business success. His practical insights and real-world experience make him a sought-after voice in both athletic and corporate environments.

Learn more about Chris at www.garnerleadership.com.

www.ingramcontent.com/pod-product-compliance
Lightning Source LLC
Chambersburg PA
CBHW021641120626
46545CB00002B/653